# How To Get Over Your Breakup

## The Definitive Guide To Recovering From A Breakup and Moving On With Life

**Rachel Adamson**

Copyright © Rachel Adamson Publishing

All rights reserved.
No part of this publication may be reproduced, distributed, or transmitted in any form or by any means, including photocopying, recording, or other electronic or mechanical methods, without the prior written permission of the publisher, except in the case of brief quotations embodied in critical reviews and certain other non-commercial uses permitted by copyright law.

# Table Of Contents

Breaking Up Is Never Easy

Breaking Up: The Basics

The Healthy Way To Start Your Recovery

The Quick Start Guide To Recovering Fast: What To Do

The Quick Start Guide To Recovering Fast: What NOT To Do

Breakup Case Study: Anna

Coping With The Grief of a Breakup

The Stages of a Breakup and How To Handle Them

Protecting Yourself 101

The 4 Rules of Disengagement and How To Stick To Them

Breakup Case Study: Scott

Dealing With The Horrible Emotions

Breakup Case Study: Therese

Moving On With Your Life!

# Breaking Up Is Never Easy

*"Nothing in the universe can stop you from letting go and starting over."*
**Guy Finley**

No one ever said that going through a break-up was easy. When you are forced to say goodbye to someone you thought you would have in your life forever, it hurts, no matter what side of the break-up you're on. But despite enduring the pain of letting go, a break-up does not have to break you. Yes, your relationship has broken down, but you are not broken and you will get through this. Unfortunately, the grieving process can be pretty hard going. The fact is, you have suffered a loss of something you believed in and someone that you have cared about deeply. Break-ups aren't all the same and rarely are they straight forward. You may never have to see your ex again or you may have chosen to remain friends. You may have children together or a group of shared friends. You may have to see each other at work everyday or you may only have to see each other one more time when you return each other's belongings. But no matter what your break-up looks like, it's likely to be hard to navigate from time to time.

When your heart hurts, it won't be easy to be around your ex, but it also won't be easy to be away from them. You will probably feel many emotions during your grieving period. You may volley from sadness to anger, from disappointment to self-doubt, from love to hate and back again. All of these feelings are normal when we are going through a loss. But it's how we cope with those feelings, what we *do* with them, that determines how long we will suffer and to what extent our pain will affect us. It's what we do with our emotions that determines how quickly we can bounce back. There are ways to protect yourself from added pain. There are ways to overcome your sadness. There are ways to maintain your dignity and self-respect. A break-up may feel all-consuming, but eventually, your pain will recede and you will recover.

The aim of this book is to guide you through the fastest, easiest, and most effective way to get over your break-up. It will help you to come through this difficult part of your life with your head held high, your confidence intact, and your self-beliefs unscathed. You may feel pain, but you do not have to experience devastation. You may feel disappointed, but you do not have to feel as though your relationship was a failure. No matter what the circumstances of your break-up were, this book will help you move past it. By focusing on self-care and self-protection, you will shed any negative self-beliefs that your break-up may have caused you to develop. By learning more about who you are and what your needs are, you will be able to put a stop to any negative relationship patterns you may have developed and start moving in a more positive, promising direction. By limiting your exposure to emotional triggers, you will be giving yourself time to reflect, process, and feel your feelings in a safe way. By learning to change your unhelpful behavioral habits and your harmful thought patterns, you will be setting yourself up for future relationship success. Yes, you may have to change your vision of the future. You may have to make a lot of adjustments to your life as a result of your break-up. But being single does not have to be a negative thing. No matter what the circumstances behind your break-up were, what lies in the future is completely up to you now. There is hope and there is a light at the end of this tunnel.

## Breaking Up: The Basics

Relationships should be a place where we can be our true selves without fear of rejection. They should be a space that is safe from pain, betrayal, and self-doubt. They should make us feel good about ourselves and the world around us. They should make us feel loved and free to love in return. Relationships should be a place of open honesty. They should be based on trust, intimacy, and mutual respect. But not all relationships fit within these ideals. Sure, all relationships have ups and downs. No two people can go through life without experiencing disagreements and times of trouble. Negative things do happen in life and when they do, it's the people that are closest to us that bear the brunt of our ill feelings. We, in turn, provide the same safe space for our partners. When times are hard, it's natural for a relationship to become strained. So too, changes within a household can have negative effects on a relationship. Having a new baby, going through financial difficulties, falling ill, or any number of other major life changes will naturally affect the health of our relationships. And while some couples come through their troubles triumphantly, many others simply can't make it work.

When a relationship breaks down, regardless of whose fault it is or who tries the hardest to keep things together, most people will feel as though the relationship has failed. You may feel as though you are a failure or that your ex didn't step up enough to prevent the failure. But the more you use the word *fail*, the more negativity you are adding to a problem that is painful enough as it is. We must, at all costs, resist the urge to refer to our break-ups as "failed relationships". The negativity behind those words is toxic. Believing that you have failed will not only have a negative effect on your self-esteem, but it may also cause you to form negative self-beliefs. The more you focus on *failure*, the more negative weight you are anchoring yourself down with. If you consider yourself a failure where relationships are concerned, you will be less likely to get out there and try again, and less likely to trust yourself with future relationships. But more than that, believing that you have failed is not going to help you in the here and now, and this is when it really counts.

In order to survive a break-up with your wits intact, it's imperative that you get a healthy perspective on your break-up. Is it true that any relationship that doesn't make it all the way to someone's funeral has failed? Isn't that a little dramatic? Isn't it a bit of sweeping statement to cancel out all the good in a relationship just because it didn't last forever? Does a break-up really mean that the whole relationship was a failure? That the whole thing was a waste of time? I personally, do not believe so. It is important to be able to hold onto the positive and let go of the negative. This does not mean that you should place so much focus on the positive side of your relationship with your ex that you forget why you broke up in the first place. Nor does it mean that you should jump back into a broken relationship because there were some good times. But what it does mean is that you should not beat yourself up because things didn't end well. You should not let it define how you feel about yourself or prevent you from continuing on with your life. You should not let it make you believe that you are bad at relationships or that you are hopeless. We all make mistakes. We all pick the wrong person for us from time to time. But that does not mean that we have failed. Plus, there is nothing wrong with having short-term relationships. People change a lot with time and it's only natural that some people will simply outgrow each other over the course of their relationship. Our needs, desires, and life plans will inevitably change and shift as we move through our lives, and sometimes that means growing apart from the people we love.

If you're prone to thinking of your relationship or yourself as a failure, it's time to start thinking differently. Think about some of your current or past relationship goals. Is being with someone to the end of time your only relationship goal? Probably not. Most of us have smaller goals along the way, such as developing a strong trust with someone, feeling safe with someone, sharing a home with someone, being with someone who makes us laugh, raising a pet together, being a good team, etc. Usually, when we get to the stage of breaking up, we have already reached some of our smaller goals. This means that the relationship was not one big failure. Perhaps your end goal was not reached, but surely there was some good in it. Surely some aspects of your relationship were positive. The reason I'm mentioning all of this is so that you can get a better grasp on the language you use when describing your relationship. Focusing your heart and soul on the things that went wrong will not serve you well. Sure, there will be times when you will feel low and you'll need to reflect on the things that didn't work out the way you wanted them to. We all need to mourn, and we need to be realistic about the elements of our relationships that were not so good. However, if you spend the majority of your time and mental energy focusing on all the negative things, you will be placing extra emotional weight on yourself that you simply do not need in a time of grief. Going through a loss is not easy. Reshaping your life after a break-up can be really hard going and scary. But you can make it easier for yourself by trying to keep your chin up. No, you did not get everything you wanted out of your relationship, but that does not have to dictate what your future relationships will be like. It does not define you. It does not mean that you are hopeless or tragic. It simply means that you were two people that had good times and bad times together. It means that you are human.

With this idea in mind, take a few minutes to think about some of the positive things you gained from your relationship. Resist the urge to become overly sentimental or to dwell on things that will cause you emotional pain. Think instead about things that you have learned from your relationship that will help you in the future. For instance, did you learn anything about yourself? Do you have any needs that were or were not met by your ex? Perhaps you realized that you need more personal space than your relationship allowed for. Or maybe you would prefer more intimacy and trust in future relationships. You may have found that you need to be with someone who is more supportive of your endeavors or someone who is less involved with your personal projects. You might like to live with someone who's willing to divide household duties more evenly. You may have found that you struggled to maintain your sense of autonomy in your relationship, that your ex-partner was overbearing or over-involved. There are of course, endless possibilities with this, so do take the time to think about any other things I haven't listed here.

Being able to assess things like this realistically and objectively is a great way to get perspective on your relationship with your ex as well as helping you to shape your ideal future. Plus, when we focus on what we've learned and the positive things we can take out of a negative situation, we're helping ourselves to bounce back more quickly. There will always be negative thoughts that pop into your head, and that's completely natural, especially when you're feeling low. But just be mindful of how much time and energy you spend thinking about those things. Too much negative thinking can be detrimental to your mood, your self esteem, and your general mindset. It's important to learn how to protect yourself from harmful habits and negative thought patterns. This is something that I will discuss at length throughout this book, but for now, keep an eye on your thought patterns and do your best not to dwell on the things that upset you. If you struggle to do that, try to distract yourself by doing something productive or set a timer and allow yourself a set amount of time to dwell. When your alarm goes off, do your best to turn those thoughts off.

Relationships have come a long way since the days of our parents and grandparents. There have been a lot changes to the ways in which people couple up. This can be seen in some very obvious ways, such as the fact that nowadays many couples today share household duties and child-rearing responsibilities. In most relationships, both parties work to support the family. Diversity in relationships has also led to a lot positive changes in relationships in general, and we can see that many couples put a lot more thought into choosing whether or not to marry than their older relatives may have. The whole idea of the 'family unit' has been broadened. There are many ways couples can live their lives now; they do not have to abide by the laws of convention any longer if they choose not to. They do not have to have children if they don't want to. They can move in with one another as and when they please. They can focus on their education and career before settling down, etc. But along with these positive changes, new challenges have arisen. Without marriage being the end-all pivotal move of our socially expected behavior, relationships are a lot more open-ended now.

There's a lot more grey in the ways in which we couple up. There are some conflicting thoughts regarding marriage and divorce in today's world, but what we do know is that fewer people are getting married each year in the United States, and those that do marry, do so later in life than they would have a few decades ago. We know that divorce rates have been significant since the 1980's. And of course, none of us can ignore the rise in Internet dating.

Today's contemporary women are not necessarily being raised with marriage as their key goal in life. These days, it has become more socially acceptable for both women and men of all sexualities, to play the field, so to speak. We are no longer living in a culture where we have to get married young in order for our lives to be of value. But what does all this mean when it comes to breaking up? Frankly, it means that the more we date, the more break-ups we are likely to endure. This isn't a reason to stop dating or to feel like the future is grim. But rather, it's something that should encourage us to develop a thicker skin and open our minds to the possibilities of less conventional coupling. Most of us will have some trial and error where our love lives are concerned. Some of us will have to kiss a lot of frogs before we find our prince or princess.

In this regard, being able to bounce back from a break-up is a good skill to have on your side. Furthermore, it is possible that by knowing and accepting that a relationship might not last forever, we might be more appreciative of what we have both during and after our relationships. We might be less inclined to view our past relationships as failures, and more able to view them as being right at the time, just not right forever. This book is not designed to make you think a certain way or to change your hopes for the future. But it is always a good idea to reflect on what's happening for you personally in light of what's happening in a broader context; especially when times are changing.

Whatever your relationship was like, no matter how long it lasted or what the specific pros and cons there were, getting over it is going to suck a little, if you'll pardon the phrase. There is a reason so many films, books, and songs have been written about breaking up. There is a reason for the sheer quantity of love-focused art that we have all become familiar with, and that reason is that it reflects what we're all going through in real life. It tells us that we're not alone. It tells us that it's okay to feel sad, angry, and lonely. But it also tells us that we can carry on when things don't go our way, and we will. Endings are one of the hardest things we have to cope with as human beings. Loss is not easy. Grief is not easy. But human beings are incredibly resilient and that's what we need to hold onto after a break-up. All of our sufferings will get easier with time. But in the meantime, we have to do everything we possibly can to keep our wits about us and keep believing, hoping, and trying for a happier future.

We have to be able to protect ourselves emotionally. We have to think more deeply about our relationship patterns so that we can make necessary changes before trying again. We have to shift our focus onto the things that bring us joy, confidence, and feelings of accomplishment, rather than allowing ourselves to dwell on all the things that have gone wrong in our lives. These things take practice, and you must be patient with yourself. Time always plays a part in these things so try to keep that in mind when you don't feel like you're recovering as quickly as you should be. Every person and every relationship is different, grieving periods will vary, but for now, remember that it's okay to mourn. Focus on treating yourself kindly and doing everything you can to move forward for now. Just don't put too much pressure on yourself. Easy does it.

## The Healthy Way To Start Your Recovery

Getting over a break-up isn't something that happens overnight. Over time, you will need to feel your feelings and grieve the loss of your relationship. After that, you will be able to get back up and build a new life for yourself. This book will guide you through the grieving process in the easiest and most effective manner, but in the meantime, it's important to get a grasp on harmful behaviors that could make getting over your ex a lot harder than it needs to be. In order to avoid getting swept away in the tide of your break-up, have a look at the following list of essential do's and don't's to keep yourself on the right track. Start putting these ideas into action right away so that you can make things as easy as possible for yourself.

Remember that breaking up is painful, but it doesn't have to be excruciating. It is natural to feel devastated or lost after a big change in life, but there are things that you can do to take the sting out of the feelings you're having right now. It's important that you do everything you can to ease your pain; only you can do that for yourself. You will have a chance to think a lot more deeply about yourself in the wake of your break-up as this book progresses, but it is my firm belief the sooner you get started, the easier things will be for you. So try to implement these rules in your life as soon as you can. If some topics listed here are not relevant to you and your ex, feel free to move on to the next thing. It would be naive to assume that everyone is going to face the same exact challenges so feel free to take whatever advice you feel is relevant to you and disregard the rest.

# The Quick Start Guide To Recovering Fast: What To Do

## Get Some Space

After a break-up, many people feel daunted by the idea of getting space. It's natural to feel lonely or uncomfortable being alone, especially if you had been living with your ex before your break-up. If you and your partner were the type of couple that did everything together, it's very possible that you will feel a bit out of place when you're on your own. But taking time to get your head cleared is important for everyone after a break-up. Your mind needs time and space to breathe and put things back in order. Being around your ex in the early stages of your break-up can make things confusing and a lot more painful than they need to be. It's very hard to think clearly about someone when you're subject to constant reminders of them. Even if you're not seeing your ex, it's important that you cut off communication for a while in the early stages of your break-up. Texting, emailing, and talking on the phone with your ex is not going to allow you the space you need to make sense of things and adjust to the change in your life. It's like trying to tie your shoes with one hand behind your back. How can you begin to get over someone if you're still talking to them all the time? How can you adjust to single life with a constant reminder of being coupled up? It can be torturous to be around your ex in the aftermath of a break-up, so spare yourself that torture by stepping back for a while.

For couples who choose to remain friends, or couples who will have to see each other due to work, children, or any other shared obligations, taking a few weeks away from one another is equally important. Space doesn't need to last forever if you don't want it to, but it's important that you give yourself time to feel your feelings and get used to flying solo before striking up a friendship or continuing communication with your ex. You need to give yourself a chance to grieve and get refocused. If you're going to remain friends, you have to let one relationship end before you can start a new relationship under new constructs. So if you are newly broken up, or if you broke up a while ago and just haven't recovered yet, do what you can to get some space away from your ex. Let go of communication with them for a little while. Resist the urge to check out their social media profiles or attend events where you know they'll be. Resist the urge to text when you're feeling lonely or when you're reminded of something you'd normally share with them. When you're in the acute stages of loss you don't need extra reminders to ramp up your emotional pain. This doesn't have to be forever, it's just a way to limit emotional distractions while times are tough.

**Stop Fighting**
There comes a time in every relationship when it's time to stop fighting, and if you've broken up with your partner, that time is now. All couples are different; some are fighters and some are not. But whether you and your ex have always fought or you just started fighting recently, you have to know when to let go. The more we argue, the more we will feel emotionally activated and exhausted. During and after a break-up, emotions are already going to be running high, and for most people, anger will play a part in that. But fighting can be cyclical and pointless. What it does is maintain anger as the primary emotion of the break-up. This not only causes people to feel drained and on edge, but it also can prevent you from feeling your deeper feelings of sadness and loss. The problem with this is that the longer you remain out of touch with your deeper feelings, the longer your recovery may be and the more taxing your break-up will be in general. If you find that you and your partner are fighting about things that are unlikely to ever be resolved, you have to know when to walk away. A good way to think of this is to ask yourself if you want to *win* the fight or if you want the fight to *end*.

Ask yourself how important what you're fighting about really is.
Are you fighting because something needs to be resolved?
Or are you fighting because emotions are high?
Do you just want the last word?
Are you going to gain anything positive from this fight?
Is fighting making anything better?

It takes a big person to step back from an argument, but often, that's what it takes to make the fighting stop. Someone has to be the bigger person, put down their verbal weapons, and agree to disagree. When we make the decision to let go of the tension between ourselves and our exes, we will be free to start getting over the break-up and moving on with our lives. It's not always an easy thing to imagine - the idea of moving on - it can be daunting and scary. And if that is the case, perhaps it's worth asking yourself if you're fighting because you just don't want to let go. It's okay if that is what's beneath it all. It's natural for us to cling to the things we're most familiar with. Moving on is a big deal, it means finding your feet on new ground. But deep down we all know that arguing with our ex will not turn back time or make things any easier. The process of starting over again is going to be challenging, but you can do this. Take the first step towards your new future by stopping the fight as soon as you can.

**Try to talk about other things.**
At one time or another, we've all been, or at least known, the person who talks incessantly about their ex. No matter where you are or who you're with, somehow the conversation always comes back to the break-up. The fact is, a break-up can be all consuming. No matter how long you were together or what your relationship was like, endings are hard. They can take over your mind *and* your mouth. In general, there is nothing wrong with talking about your break-up. Your friends and family are there to listen and be supportive. You will need to get things off your chest. But if you're not careful, you may find that little time passes without you mentioning your ex. There are a few problems when it comes to talking about your ex too much. First of all, it prevents you from thinking about other things, including having fun and blowing off steam. It prevents you from getting relief from your pain and can make it hard to enjoy the positive things in your life.

Remember that you need to get some head space from your partner and your break-up in general. Your mind needs a break from all the anguish you're feeling. If your thoughts are so deeply rooted in your break-up, you might have a hard time concentrating at work or the standard of your work could drop. Furthermore, when you talk about the same thing over and over again, eventually, no matter how much they care about you, your friends will tire of it. This could mean isolating yourself and reducing your support network. It can be quite draining for a friend or loved one to listen to the same thing on repeat. It's not that people don't care, but if you can only play one note on a piano, it's bound to start sounding monotonous after a while. There has to be a way of measuring how much you talk about your ex, otherwise, you risk alienating yourself from the people around you and holding yourself back.

So ask yourself now if you have become the person that can't stop talking about their ex. If you think you do talk a little too much about the break-up, chances are you're thinking about it more than you need to be. It's not going to be easy to distract yourself from those thoughts. But you have to do your best to focus on other things as much as you can. There will be plenty of time to feel your pain, but it needs to be balanced out so that you don't drown in it. Ask your friends to let you know when you're talking about your break-up too much so that they can help gently redirect the conversation. Focus on listening to other things people are talking about when you have a hard time changing the subject, and try to join in and really engage with any other topics at hand. This is a good way to distract you from obsessive thinking and show your friends that you appreciate them being there for you.

Remember that it's always okay to talk about what's going on in your life, you just have to be mindful of when to give yourself a break. Usually, when someone talks incessantly about something, the conversation never reaches a resolution. The same thoughts and feelings will come up again and again, but they never actually go anywhere. This is tiring for everyone involved, including yourself. If this is something that you think might be happening with you right now, don't beat yourself up about it. It can be really hard to think of other things when you're feeling low. Just do your best to focus on other things as and when you can. Try to give you mind some relief from all that weight every once in a while.

**Focus on yourself.**
Breaking up with someone can be a blessing in disguise. A lot of times when we're in an intimate relationship, we give all of our energy and attention to our partner. This can be a hard habit to break, which means that many people continue to focus on their ex even

after the relationship has ended. This can manifest in many ways from worrying about how your ex is doing to being consumed with anger towards them, and everything in between. But again, when all of your focus and attention is facing outward, you might be neglecting what's happening inside you. The less attention you offer yourself, the longer it will take to process your feelings. Furthermore, there comes a point when you simply have to redirect your attention. If you are worried about your ex, you have to try to let go of that. Your ex is an adult, and what's happening for them is their business now.

Making that cut can be especially hard if you were the one who kept things together before the break-up. If you're used to caring for someone (or everyone in your life), training yourself to stop doing that won't be easy. You may have to remind yourself of this a lot in the beginning because kicking old habits does take persistence. In order to rewrite overactive care-taking tendencies, you'll have to get used to recognizing when you're placing too much focus on other people and too little on yourself. Each time you recognize that behavior resurfacing, you've got to tell yourself to stop that thought process and focus your attention elsewhere. If you hear yourself telling people that you are worried about your ex or that you feel bad for them because "no one else knows them like you do" or other similar phrases, be firm with yourself. Tell yourself to stop that thought process and get a healthier, more self-focused, mindset. The thing is, you don't have to become cold-hearted in order to focus on yourself.

You don't have to stop caring about other people. You just have to learn how to measure that care for others in a way that will not distort the reality of the situation nor impede on your own need for self-care, self-love, and emotional attention. Being self-focused during difficult times does not make you a bad person. Focusing on your ex's wellbeing will only make you feel guilty or sympathetic towards them when you need to get space. This could mean helping your ex get over the break-up while you remain static in your own recovery. At the end of the day, the more energy you can spend on *you*, the quicker your recovery will be.

In addition, if you are feeling intense negative emotions toward your ex, such as being overcome with anger, spite, disappointment or jealousy, you'll have to do what you can to soften those feelings so that you can focus on you. When we are overcome with thoughts and feelings about someone else, we can get into cyclical thought patterns that never really come to a resolution. For instance, you might find that you remain angry about specific things that happened between you and your ex, yet you never really come to the end of those feelings. Those thoughts never really go anywhere productive. And if your negative thoughts never come to a resolution, you can drive yourself crazy by placing too much focus on them. Some things simply will not be resolved because there's nothing else you can do about them. They may just have to be left as they are. And when that is the case, the only thing you can control is the effect those things are having on *you*.

If you can't change what has happened, why continue beating your head against that particular brick wall? Because you do have some power where things like this are concerned. What you can *do* is focus on yourself instead, so that you can at least temper the impact those things are having on you.

So what does it look like to focus on you? First of all, it means taking good care of yourself physically and emotionally. Yes, you might go out on a bender after the break-up and your routine may become temporarily dismantled. These are normal things that are to be expected. But there will come a point when it's time to pull it together. You can make things easier on yourself by taking good care of yourself. Eat well and get plenty of rest and exercise. Try not to drown your sorrows in alcohol or drugs and try to keep your behavior from veering into recklessness. Do nice things for yourself on a daily basis. Buy yourself something nice with all the money you'll save on birthdays and Valentine's day gifts. Meet up with friends who you haven't managed to see for a while because your relationship took up all your time. Take a hot bath or a nice walk on the beach or in the park when you find yourself at a loose end.

Most importantly, listen to your thoughts and feelings. Sit quietly for ten minutes to an hour every day and let your feelings come to the surface. Consider them and allow yourself to feel your emotions. Allow yourself to cry. Don't place blame on yourself or anyone else, just let yourself feel. Then treat yourself with even more kindness. These are extremely important things to do in times of loss. Being kind to yourself should be non-negotiable. Treat yourself like you would treat a friend. Go easy on yourself and give yourself the attention you need right now.

**Be social.**
For most people, facing the public after a break-up can be really hard going. When you're out, people will unknowingly ask how your partner or how your children are doing and you will have to have the awkward we-broke-up conversation. Unfortunately, without making a major public announcement on network TV, these awkward moments are relatively unavoidable. They will happen. Things may be further complicated if you and your ex have shared friends. Your friends may not want to take sides or they might feel uncomfortable talking about your break-up. These things are to be expected. But none of these potentialities are worth hiding in your bedroom alone waiting until the storm passes. If for no other reason, you deserve to go out and have fun. You deserve to see your friends and get some lightness in your life.

There are many people in the world that choose to suffer in silence, and there's nothing wrong with that. But you have to be careful that you don't isolate yourself at a time when you need to be around people who care about you. You don't have to go out every night of the week, but staying social and getting out could prevent you from spending too much time alone and ending up spiraling into damaging thought patterns. If you have experienced depression at any time in your life, you will need to be mindful of any inclination you have to hide away. Too much time alone can be dangerous for anyone's mood when they're going through a tough time, so getting out and seeing your friends and family is a necessity when going through a loss. You need to be able to see the people that are still in your life. You might want to reconnect with someone you've lost touch with or use your new found freedom to go out to an event that your ex wouldn't have enjoyed and meet some new people.

If you find that your spirits drop in the afternoon, spend your lunch hour with a friend or colleague to avoid getting into a slump at work. Finally, if you need to talk to someone, reach out. Call a friend who you trust and get it all off your chest. All human beings need an outlet. We all need to be released from our weighty emotions from time to time. Just use care when deciding who to confide in. Try not to talk to people who are likely to be insensitive or uncaring. Rather, when you need to talk, flock to the people who support you and make you feel good about the world.

**Hide the evidence.**
Depending on the length of time you were with your ex and whether or not you shared a home with them, you're likely to have some things around the house that remind you of them. When you're in a heightened emotional state, reminders of your ex can be tormenting. So you have to do what you can to protect yourself from the objects forcing you to think about your break-up. Start by getting rid of anything you can. If you have bedsheets that still smell like your ex, get rid of them and buy yourself a nice new set of sheets that are all yours. If you have a box of your ex's belongings, give it back as soon as possible. Set a deadline for them to collect their things, and in the meantime, put that stuff where you will not see it on a daily basis. Put pictures and sentimental things like letters and gifts away. You can get rid of them completely if that's what you want to do, but if you're not ready to take that step, put those things in a box, tape it shut and put it somewhere out of reach until you are ready to deal with it. If there are things that you bought together and you can afford to buy new ones for yourself, let your ex keep that stuff and start fresh. In the beginning, the less evidence you have around your house, the better. Stop wearing your ex's t-shirt to bed. Stop re-reading their favorite book. Stop watching the show you guys never got a chance to finish, because if you keep watching it, all you'll notice is the absence of your partner.

Protect yourself from things that will cause you to feel emotionally activated. Break-ups are hard enough without being faced with constant reminders of them. Remember that you can always go back later. You can finish that TV series and re-read that book at a later date if you really want to. But for now, give yourself some room to breathe. Give yourself a new space that is entirely yours. This way you can get used to being on your own more quickly and allow yourself to think about other things without the temptation to revisit and dwell on the past.

**Allow yourself to grieve.**
Grief is one of the hardest things human beings have to go through in life. Endings are hard. Losing someone you care about can feel torturous. It can feel like you're drenched in sadness. It can make you question yourself and your future. It can be frightening and sad. Unfortunately, there is no quick fix for grief. Everyone will experience it differently. There is no set amount of time for grief and no rules. However, grief will hang around longer if you don't allow yourself to recognize it. It's natural to want to distract yourself when you're feeling down. And there are certainly times when it's necessary to do so, as I've already mentioned. But attempting to distract yourself *all the time* will only lengthen your grieving period. Later in this book, you will read an entire chapter dedicated to helping you through the grieving process. But for now, keep in mind that your feelings just want to be felt. That means you will probably have to cry. You may feel anger or rage. You may feel defeat. You may feel as though you have failed or as though the future is hopeless.

As long as you maintain perspective on those thoughts, you will get past them. With each cry, you will be closer to the end of it. Try not to get swept away with grief. Don't let it rule your mind or change your self-beliefs. But accept that you are coping with a loss and there will be difficult emotions attached to that. If you listen to your feelings they will pass far easier than if you ignore them. For this reason, be careful about what you do during your grieving period. Try not to go off the rails or self-destruct.

Remember that this break-up is not who you are, it's just something you're going through right now. This event in your life does not define you. It's just where you happen to be at the time. It will pass. The best thing you can do is try to be patient. Try to accept that you'll be feeling a little up and down over the next few weeks or even months. Go easy on yourself. Don't get angry with yourself if you don't get over it right away. Don't beat yourself up for feeling sad. Even if you were the one who initiated the break-up, grief will be a part of it. Treat yourself kindly during this time. Listen to your thoughts and try to take one day at a time.

**Be mature.**
This book is not designed to be strict, bossy, or overly harsh on you. It is meant to cover as many possible break-up difficulties as possible so that you can find the advice relevant to you and your situation. So if you read a section that you feel does not apply to you, move on to the next one that does. That being said, I could not write this book without mentioning the fact that playing games and acting a fool will not make your break-up any easier to cope with. This includes posting things on social media for the sheer purpose of making your ex jealous. It includes gossiping or saying nasty things about your ex to their friends or your mutual friends. It includes any method of "getting back" at them. And it includes texting or calling them for no good reason after you have split up. If you're planning on going out drinking and you're likely to drunk dial, give your phone to a friend who you can trust to keep you right.

The problem with behaviors like this is that they will not help relations with your ex and they're usually things that you'll regret after the fact. That means giving yourself even more to be upset about in the long run. It also could prolong your angst. If you send a drunken text and get no reply, how are you going to feel about that in the morning? If you're playing games with your ex, where do you see that behavior going in the long run? Is it going to have a positive effect on anything? Or is it just going to make things messier? We've all done things that we wish we hadn't, but if we think about this stuff now, when we're sober and level-headed, we might be able to prevent ourselves from repeating those mistakes. Try not to act out if your ex rebounds quickly. Try to keep your jealousy and cruel comments at bay. Try not to play games. At the end of the day, try to be your best self. That way you can look back and feel good about how you got through your break-up rather than being left with regret and a sour taste in your mouth. No one needs more embarrassing moments to regret. Sure, you may fall out of line here and there.

Grief can bring out the worst in us, and that's okay. Just do your best to stay in charge of your actions.

If you know that alcohol brings out the worst in you, consider not drinking for a while. If you're tempted to do something of questionable judgment on social media, take a break from life online for a while. If you think you're likely to text your ex when you shouldn't, delete their number or have someone hide your phone until the moment passes. Remember, no one ever regrets being the bigger person.

## The Quick Start Guide To Recovering Fast: What Not To Do

**Do not stalk your ex or their new partner.**
I really cannot stress this enough, stalking your ex in person or online is harmful behavior on many levels. Online stalking is a major temptation for many people going through a break-up, and it's not hard to see why. For those who use social media, having the ability to "check up" on your ex can be seriously hard to resist. It's like having the key to a mysterious locked door and resisting the temptation to open it.

But you have to ask yourself, if you let temptation win, what are you really going to get out of this? How are you going to feel if you see something you don't want to see? What is it going to feel like to see your ex having a great time out with their friends on a night that you're home alone watching rom-coms? How will it feel to see that they've moved on? More importantly, social media does not show the whole picture. Your ex might be consciously displaying their life in a certain way in an effort to save face or even make you jealous. Stalking them might just be giving in exactly what they're trying to deliver to you.

For a lot of people, it is anger and spite that drives them to stalk. On some level, they want to feel enraged. They want to be justified in feeling angry and hurt. But you have to remember, are already are justified in those feelings. You're allowed to feel negatively towards your ex without seeking any more reasons for those feelings. If you give in to the inclination to stalk your ex, who's the one that's really going to suffer for it? Most likely, you are. However, if you're able to shift your focus away from your ex and their post-break-up behavior, and focus instead on protecting yourself, your break-up will be a lot easier to handle.

The thing is, regardless of what you see online, both you and your ex are going through a loss. And it is likely that the two of you may cope with that loss in different ways. If your ex is out partying a lot or rebounding, or even jumping into a new relationship, you have to tell yourself that none of that is any of your business anymore. No one needs reminders of things like that. No one needs the added pain of watching their ex from afar. This is one of the first steps in learning how to focus on *you*. It isn't easy to step back from your ex, but there are ways to do so that are less destructive than others. When you focus on yourself, you're giving yourself a chance to practice caring about *you*. You're giving yourself time to grieve. Stalking is a pretty easy way to add time and pain to your grieving process.

No, it will not be easy to not see your ex every day. But it will be a lot harder if you have to see them moving on. The other thing to remember is that what people put online is their choice. So even if they're posting a bunch of pictures of them out having a great time, that doesn't mean that they're not hurting for the other 22 hours of the day.

Why torture yourself by checking up on them and being forced to see all their happiest post-break-up moments? Similarly, how will you feel if you see that your ex seems to be falling apart? Imagine the difficult emotions you'd have to cope with if that were the case. Some things are just better left in the dark. The best thing you can do is unfollow, unfriend, or change your social media settings so that their posts will not come up in your feed. If you are planning on staying friends with your ex, you can always undo these settings in the future after you've healed. Remember that nothing is forever. The acute stage after a break-up can be agonizing and it can feel all-encompassing. But things will ease up sooner than you think. So focus on doing what you can do *now* to make things easier on yourself.

Just to be clear, this advice extends beyond social media. Driving by your ex's house to see what they're up to should also be off limits. Even they live on your daily commute, consider taking a different route to work until the dust settles so that you can be free of added pain. Similarly, try not to attend events or go places where you know your ex will be. There will be times when this is avoidable such as being invited to a mutual friend's wedding or other similar events. But beyond that, do what you can to not be where they are for a while.

Don't go somewhere just so you can catch a glimpse of them. Because, when two exes see each other out, not only can it be awkward and painful, but it's also possible to end up in a silent battle of who's having a better time. It can get childish, and if alcohol is involved, it could end up getting ugly. Remember that you don't have to avoid your ex forever. Just do what you can during the acute stages of this loss to protect yourself from harmful behaviors. Don't text them or ask your friends to check up on them. When you find yourself wondering what your ex is up to, try to shift your focus gently back to yourself. There will be plenty of time in the future - after you have healed - to find out what they are up to if you really want to know. For now, consider stalking off limits.

**Don't make any major life changing decisions.**
A lot of times when we're going through a period of loss and transition, we cope with it by distracting ourselves with new projects. In theory, there is nothing wrong with this coping mechanism at all. In times of change and emotional stress, it's great to have something else to focus on. Especially if that thing is something positive such as taking up a new hobby, taking a class in the evenings, or embarking on a fitness journey. But you have to be careful not to make changes that are too drastic, such as deciding to quit your job without a back-up plan or making expensive purchases when your finances are already thinly stretched.

It's easy for the mind to get swept away and to think with limited clarity when everything feels like it's falling down around you. But it's important to keep your head screwed on and not get swept away in post-break-up extravagance. The last thing anyone needs after a break-up is to be hit with bank-breaking bills or to regret making irreversible split decisions. It's vital to maintain some balance and keep your actions measured.

Yes, there are times when the right decision will be to pick up and move. There are times when getting a puppy is exactly what you need. But you have to be realistic when making major life changes. You have to make sure that you're making decisions because you have the resources to back them up and you genuinely believe them to be appropriate choices. You need to be close to positive that you will proudly stand by your decisions long after this acute period of transition. So when you feel yourself pondering big changes to implement in your life, try to think long-term so that you're not setting yourself up for a fall. For instance, maybe you won't actually have the time and money to raise a puppy right now, but you could afford to join a local "borrow my dog" group to satisfy your need for doggy cuddles.

If you shared a home with your ex, maybe moving to a new house isn't entirely feasible right now, but that doesn't mean you can't redecorate to make the place feel like it's yours. It might not be wise to quit your job right now, but maybe you can afford to take a little vacation. You get the gist. Be careful with sweeping statements and split decisions. Times of transition are never easy, and doing something exciting and new could be just what the doctor ordered. However, you might be able to achieve that with something as simple a makeover or a few new articles of clothing, rather than splashing out on a new car. When making post-break-up decisions, always ask yourself if this is something you may regret later on.

**Don't obsess over texts and emails.**
This is something that I will mention a few times throughout this book, and for good reason. It is extremely common for people to read texts and emails from their ex over and over again, picking them apart and obsessing over them. You might keep looking at

them and derive a different meaning each time. You might ponder them many times throughout the day. You might show them to all of your friends, either to get their opinion on them or just as part of your conversations. But behavior like can be seriously emotionally dangerous because what you're doing when you re-read your text based communications with your ex, is reliving each painful moment on repeat. By clinging to these texts, you are clinging to your break-up pain. You are feeding all your negative emotions and effectively torturing yourself.

Don't get me wrong, it is not easy for everyone to step away from their phones. As a culture in general, we are more attached to our electronic devices these days than ever before. Even leaving your phone in the house while you take a ten-minute walk to the store could feel excruciating. Many people can't even go to the bathroom without bringing their phone with them. And because of this change in how we communicate, most of us have detailed records of our conversations in our possession, for better or worse.

Back in the days when the majority of our conversations were had in person or on the phone, the temptation to relive those conversations was a lot easier to resist because all we had to go on were our own memories. Now we can carry those conversations around with us literally everywhere we go. It's dangerous. And again, it all comes down to protecting yourself. Allowing yourself to become attached to the conversations you've had with your ex (or other people who may have inside information about your break-up) means holding onto the past and resisting positive forward thinking.

As painful and fresh as it all is right now, you do have the power to recover, and you can help yourself by starting to let go of the text evidence. Looking over old texts, talking about them, showing them to people, writing out your story with your ex… all of these things are keeping you glued to the spot, on an emotional level. Even when you think you're using them as a means to feel justified or as proof that you were right all along, you will not be helping yourself. Remember that it's okay to talk about what you're going through. It's okay that your thoughts will return to it again and again. And it's okay to grieve. But if you want to heal, you have to be careful with any tendencies you may have to obsess over things.

Obsessions can make us behave in ways we could later regret. They can make us unable to think about or do anything else, including moving on. So if you want a faster recovery from the pain you're feeling right now, consider deleting the texts and emails that you are clinging to. This may be hard because doing this can feel like you're officially letting go of any hope of a future with your ex. It can hurt because it feels like you're taking another step away from your ex. However, if you do not feel ready to delete those texts and emails yet, another thing you can do is to have a friend or family member take your phone for a few hours each day so that you can get some relief from it. You could also go out and leave your phone at home once or twice a day. This is likely to feel pretty strange if you usually have your phone with you everywhere you go, but you will probably find that the more you practice being away from your phone, the more you will begin to feel liberated from it. Not having your phone also allows you to process your thoughts and feelings without distraction. It can help you to recover faster and discover a sense of inner peace sooner than you would otherwise.

Of course, if you're not ready to take any of these steps, why not copy and paste your old texts and emails and put them somewhere safe for a while where you will not be reminded of them on a daily basis. You could put them in a folder on your computer or on a memory stick and then delete them from your phone so that at least you won't be forced to see them every day. Do what works for you. Just remember that the aim is to make things as easy on yourself as possible, so do whatever you can to better care for your emotional well-being by limiting your exposure to emotional triggers. Do whatever you can to let go of those texts.

**Try not to jump into another relationship right away.**
Later in this book, you will find a chapter dedicated solely to the complex world of rebounds, but for now, take extra care when thinking about diving into a new relationship in the wake of your break-up. When it comes to processing and recovering from a major change, we have to go easy on ourselves. Even if you were the one

who ended the relationship, taking some time to be on your own for a while is usually a good move.

Getting time to reflect on your relationship is really important when it comes to emotional recovery and preventing relationship difficulties from becoming a pattern in your life. After a break-up, if you give yourself time to really consider what went wrong and what it is that you really need from future relationships, you're less likely to end up in the same position later.

Furthermore, if you jump straight into a new relationship after a break-up, you could be bringing all your discontentment and pain with you. This could mean starting off on a bad foot. If you are dating someone new or considering dating someone, do your best to take things slowly. Try to take the urgency out of it and remind yourself that if there is a spark between you and this new person, it will probably still be there in a few weeks or a few months. And if they feel the same way about you, they should be willing to give you a little time. Jumping into a new relationship is a lot like making a major decision when emotions are high, and that's something you're probably better off avoiding. This is not to say that having a new, healthy relationship can't be done, but rather that it's an awful lot to put on yourself amidst the grieving process. It could mean adding further complication to a situation that's already complicated.

You will read plenty about healthy rebound behaviors later, but for now, just remind yourself to take things slow and steady. If you are already at the start of a new relationship, try to pump the breaks a little and make sure that you're getting plenty of time alone so that you can get through your difficult emotions without them eating away at you and influencing your new relationship. Remember that there's no rush and that it is okay to focus on yourself for a while. If someone new is going to be a good partner to you, they will give you the space you need right now.

**Don't blame yourself for everything.**
There are two sides to every story and the blame game rarely works out well. This is true when it comes to blaming your ex for everything that went wrong in your relationship, but it can be even

worse if you decide to take all the blame for yourself. Beating yourself up, being angry at yourself, letting yourself become overwhelmed by regrets… none of these things are going to change what has already happened. If you have a tendency to blame yourself when things go wrong, this is something to be mindful of throughout your journey to recovery. Similarly, if you have been in a relationship that was abusive or your ex-partner had a tendency to blame you or put you down when things went wrong, you will need to be extremely gentle with yourself from this point on. The problem with self-blame is that it can lead directly to self-loathing and that's really emotionally dangerous ground to be on during a time of change.

It can be very hard to move forward when you are filled with regret. But the thing is, what has passed is now in the past. There is nothing you can do to change things that have already happened. And chances are, if you did do something that you need to apologize for, you probably already have; in which case, all you can do is forgive yourself and move on. When we hold on to regret, we are holding on to the past. We are holding onto our failures and defeats instead of holding onto our triumphs and good deeds. When times are tough, we have to be our own best friends. We can't afford to continue to beat ourselves up when we're already down.

You have to remember that there were two people in your relationship. And for whatever reason, the match just wasn't right. Maybe you did something that added to the break-up, maybe your ex did, or maybe you both did. But at the end of the day, none of that matters anymore. If it wasn't that, it probably would've been something else. The best we can ever do is apologize and try to do better next time. Being overly harsh on yourself isn't necessary and it will only make things worse. Try to get some perspective if you're likely to put yourself down and raise your ex up.

Were there things that your ex did that contributed to the break-up?
Were there things they could've done better too?
Isn't it human to make mistakes sometimes?
Isn't it okay to not be your best self occasionally?

Things happen. It's unfortunate that things did not work out between you and your ex, but being mean to yourself will not help matters, it will only make things harder for you. Take care and be kind to yourself.

**Don't defame your ex or their new partner.**
A break-up should not be an excuse to speak ill of your ex or spread rumors all over town. This is a delicate topic because it could make you feel a little defensive. It is natural to feel like you need to get your anger and resentment out. And of course, it's a lot better than keeping it in and letting it eat away at you. But the manner in which you do so is what matters here. Talking to a close friend or family member about your grievances is a safe and positive way to free yourself from your negative feelings. Writing down the things that you're angry about and then burning them could also help, as would writing a letter to your ex and ripping it up instead of sending it to them.

Another productive way to process your negativity is to write a list of things that you'd like to be different in your next relationship. You might write a list of things that you won't stand for next time or personality traits that you will shield yourself from in the future. But however you choose to process your negative feelings about your ex, try to take the high road. Yes, sometimes you might slip up and say a few nasty things about your ex or the person they're now dating. That's natural. Just be careful about how much you do it and who you're talking to when you do. Try not to involve your mutual friends so that they don't feel uncomfortable. Try not to bad talk your ex to his friends or post nasty things about them online, even if you think you're being discreet.

Basically, before you act, ask yourself if you might feel a bit embarrassed by that action when the dust settles. Don't get angry at yourself if you do something spiteful, just try not to do it again. The aim is always to protect yourself, and in this case, that means protecting your reputation, your self-image, and how you feel about yourself in general. Being the bigger person will always feel better than delivering low blows.

**Try not to be passive aggressive or cryptic.**
After your break-up, you might still have to be in contact with your ex for a number of reasons. You might have to arrange to collect your belongings from them or you might have to see them out and about for other reasons. None of these things are particularly pleasant, but if communications with your ex are unavoidable, try to take the high road with this too. Sending messages or saying things that are cryptic or backhanded isn't necessary. Make your communications direct. Say what it is that you need to say. Otherwise, you're playing games and making things between you even less pleasant. If you need to express how you feel about the situation, go ahead and say it. You have nothing to lose at this point. Try not to get into a fight over it, but you don't have to be passive-aggressive.

You don't have to drop hints or mumble under your breath. If your ex did something that you found hurtful, just say it. Tell them how their actions have affected you and then get to the point of what you're trying to achieve. Playing games - although it sounds immature when you put it that way - is something that a lot of us do without even noticing. We use a text conversation to beat around the bush for an hour instead of just being forthright about what we're thinking. We make snide comments when it's unnecessary to do so. Communication after a break-up can be ugly.

Remember that the less complicated things are, the easier coping with your break-up will be. And the more direct you are when you have to talk to your ex, the more likely you will be to come out on top. Taking the high road feels good. But more than anything, there comes a point when enough is enough. There has been enough fighting. There has been enough pain. There have been enough disagreements. You can prevent further drama by getting to the point.

If your ex is the one who acts passively aggressively toward you, try to let it wash over you and like water off a duck's back. That's their issue, not yours. Try not to let yourself become emotionally activated by it and simply tell your ex to get to the point. If they continue to text or speak to you in a way that is unnecessarily difficult or dramatic, don't engage with it. Ask them to say what they need to say so that you can get on with your life. You don't need to endure hours of text drama when you're trying to get something done. You don't need to let yourself be treated that way. So say goodbye until they are prepared to be more direct with whatever it is that they're trying to communicate with you. None of these things are enjoyable so the simpler you can make things, the better. Keep conversations brief and remember why you're having the conversation in the first place. Try not to let a conversation veer into dangerous territory.

If you called to arrange a time to collect your belongings, don't let that call turn into another fight or a sentimental conversation. Yes, it will hurt sometimes, and you may need to take a few minutes or an hour to bounce back after a conversation with your ex. Go easy on yourself during these parts of your break-up. They can be quite unpleasant so make sure to give yourself plenty of self-care and space to wind down afterward difficult conversations. All you can do is your best so don't worry too much if you said things that you shouldn't have. These things happen. Just reflect on what went wrong and try to do better next time.

**Do not use your children as a weapon.**
This won't apply to everyone and it's relatively self-explanatory, but it must be said. If you have children with your ex, do everything in your power to keep them out of it. This is easier said than done, but it's something to keep at the forefront of your mind if children are involved. Relationships that include children are a whole different ball game. The thing is, when you have a child with someone, you will be tied to each other in some way, shape or form for the rest of your lives. When you break-up with someone that you will have to speak to regularly and occasionally see, you're actually beginning a new relationship with them under different constructs. It will take some time to establish that new relationship. You will both need to figure out how you can limit the amount of stress on both of you and your children while being able to work together as parents.

This is really complicated stuff and it won't happen overnight. But when it comes to your kids, do everything you can to shield them from the ugliness between you and your ex. This means not talking badly about your ex in front of your children. It means not fighting in front of your children. And it means not involving your children when the two of you are working out visiting arrangements. Of course, a lot of this will depend on the age of your children and the circumstances of your break-up. But do your very best to not withhold visitation for reasons that are not directly related to the emotional or physical well-being of your children. Try to be as amicable as possible, at least when the kids are around.

If either you or your ex is involved with someone new, try to talk about how that person will feature in your children's lives. Set some rules and boundaries that you can both agree on. And although your children will have opinions that need to be respectfully heard and considered, try not to make your kids decide which parent they want to be with and when, unless it is a situation where both you and your ex *honestly* do not mind who they choose. What I mean here is, if you give your child the option to choose between you and your ex, you cannot then become hurt or passive-aggressive if they choose their other parent for that day or that event. If you know that your feelings may be hurt, prevent difficulties by making arrangements between you and your ex and keep the kids out of the decision making.

Raising children with an ex is a complicated situation that you will need to address again and again as they grow up. There will be slip-ups and there will be times when everything seems to be going wrong. All you can do is your best with what you've got. When things are difficult, try to talk to someone else about what's going on before accidentally releasing that tension around your kids. And remember that sometimes it will hurt when your child chooses their other parent over you, especially if you feel that your ex is failing to care for them properly. But always remind yourself that your child is not the one that carries the blame for that. They love both of their parents, flaws and all. You might need to take some time to step away and lick your wounds, but keep in mind that in moments like that, you aren't being rejected.

You child is in a tricky predicament and they don't need the added pressure of keeping everyone happy. It's a dirty job, but unfortunately, it might be you that has to bear the brunt of it all. If your ex is doing something inappropriate or dangerous with your children, you may have to temporarily restrict visitation or seek outside council. In that event, encourage your children to talk about their feelings and be sure to reserve any judgment or personal opinions when they do. The more unified you can *all* be, the better. The easier you make things for your children, the easier things will be for everyone. But do remember to take good care of yourself and use the time your children are with your ex to treat yourself to some extra me time. Do things that you enjoy. Blow off some steam. This might actually a great way for you to start regaining some autonomy.

# Breakup Case Study: Anna

*When Gabriel left me, I honestly didn't think I would survive. I felt broken beyond belief. The pain was so bad. I hadn't seen it coming. I guess I'd been ignoring the warning signs, holding onto hope. I thought he was being distant because he was stressed out at work. I put it all down to tiredness. I guess I just didn't want to believe that there was actually a problem with us. In the first few weeks, I cried every single morning on my way to work and every single evening on the way home, as the stranger sitting beside me on the bus looked away in awkward secondhand embarrassment. I shuddered when I passed his new apartment which was cruelly sandwiched between work and home. I cried walking down the street. I cried in the grocery store, in taxis, and in public restrooms. I cried over dinner and again when I went to our bed and tried without success to get the sleep my body craved so badly.*

*I hurt so deeply that my pain became a part of me. It was like a new limb. It was with me no matter what I was doing. My smiles were a mask. Every action took effort. Going to work and talking to clients and colleagues was torture. I seemed to constantly be trying to cover up the fact that I'd been crying. I just couldn't stop feeling the void, the loss, the shame, the rejection of the person I cared for most. And I hate to say that that's what my life was like for months on end. It was hell. It felt like I was having constant growing pains. And in a way, I guess I was. Because it took a lot of personal growth for me to finally shed that pain and realize that I could exist happily on my own.*

*I was devastated. In the beginning, I truly did not know if I could get through it. I'd always thought Gabe was The One. I'd had so much hope for a future with this man that I was blind to all the signs. I'd believed - or at least I'd hoped - that we could overcome all the things keeping us apart. I hoped that one day he would magically realize that he loved me as much as I loved him. But he never did. And when the hope was gone, I felt flattened as if by an immeasurable force. My hope was obliterated. My vision for us, shattered. My love, named and shamed.*

*All that time, I was lost. I didn't know how to be alone. I felt like a failure. I had been rejected and that left me feeling unworthy of love. But eventually, I realized that all my energy was being directed at Gabe when I needed to focus on me. I was so caught up in the absence of him, that I was living an absence of me. I needed to learn how to be myself again. I needed to find out who I really was. Our relationship had been long, it had taken up most of my twenties. And even though we'd only lived together for the final four years of our relationship, it took a quite while to get used to living by myself again. I had really bad anxiety at the start of it. I didn't feel safe in the house by myself. But that got easier with time and eventually, I actually started enjoying it. I redecorated and started having parties again. My friendships started to bloom and grow stronger. During the time I was with Gabe, I had stopped going out and socializing with my friends, and being single gave me a chance to start having fun again. Eventually, I realized that not only could I endure single life, but that it actually worked really well for me. And it wasn't long until the tears finally dried up.*

*It's been three years since the break-up now. And although I did date a little bit during the first year, I ended up deciding to remain single for a while. It's nice to be in charge of my own life. I'm a lot more confident now than I've ever been. And all this time alone has made me so much more secure in who I am. I know what it is that I need and want from a future relationship. I am open to the idea of a new love, but I'm happy to say that I know now, that even if the next one doesn't work out, I will get through it, and that's all because I've learned how to focus on myself.*

# Coping With The Grief of a Breakup

In the aftermath of a break-up, life can be extremely difficult. Your emotions are likely to be all over the place. You might have trouble sleeping, your appetite may come and go, you may feel disoriented or dazed. Many people associate the word *grief* with death. But grief does not exclusively belong to death. Human beings can enter periods of grief after going through a loss of any kind. The loss of one's job, the loss of hope for the future, the onset of a serious illness, and of course the loss of a relationship are just a few examples of this. If you are feeling particularly floored by your break-up, you may feel ashamed or childish for being in so much pain, but there is no reason to be down on yourself. Grief affects everyone in different ways, some to greater extents than others. If you are particularly sensitive, if you've gone through a lot of break-ups in the past, if you trusted your ex and you were let down, or if you expected to be with your ex forever, it's only natural that you will feel beaten down by the ending of your relationship.

Although the main stages of grief are similar for most people, the length of time one grieves and the extent to which their grief affects their life will naturally vary between people and circumstances. The ending of a longer relationship may cause a longer grieving time than a shorter one, but this is by all means not always the case. No one knows for certain how long a period of grief will last, and having that unknown expiration date for our emotional pain does not help things. In a way, if we all knew exactly when we would start feeling better, grief would be a lot easier to handle. You could count it down on a calendar. You could start planning your life again. You'd have something to look forward to. But grieving is more like being trapped in a thick fog. When you're in it, it's hard to see in front of you or behind you. All you can do is push yourself to keep walking in any given direction and just hope that you're going the right way. But even though you might not be able to see the end of it, you know in your heart that it will not last forever. The fog will eventually lift. Things will start looking clearer again. The world will regain its color. You will feel released.

Although going through a break-up is certainly not on par with the death of a loved one, it is a loss nonetheless. It is a loss not only of your relationship, but also your plan for the future and possibly even the loss of hope. If you have children, a break-up could mean losing your established family structure. And many times, a break-up means losing your best friend to some extent. So despite the fact that you have not undergone a loss by death, the stages of grief may be quite similar. This is not to downplay what it's like to lose someone via death, nor is it to blow your break-up out of proportion. Rather, it is to better understand what you are thinking and feeling so that you can cope better and recover more easily. Have a look at the following rundown of the stages of grief and think about where you are right now and/or where you have been up to now.

Unfortunately, these stages are not going to be exactly the same for everyone and the length of time you spend on each stage will depend on you and your personal circumstances. Most people will also find that the stages overlap here and there. You may go back and forth a few times before fully getting over a stage. Progression and regression are to be expected. So look at this as a guide to better understand what you're coping with and what to expect.

## The Stages of a Breakup and How To Handle Them

### Stage 1: Denial

Denial is a word that most people think of as having a negative connotation. We think of it as a way for people to deny reality or prevent themselves from moving forward in life. We think of it as a way for people to lie to themselves about what's really going on in their lives. But denial doesn't have to be such a bad word because it does have its uses. When it comes to post-break-up grief, denial serves as a way for you to pace yourself, emotionally speaking. It is a way for your mind to cope with what's happening in your life and lessen the impact it has on you. Think about it, there are many facets to breaking up, and many big changes to adjust to. There are feelings of rejection and fear. There is loss and anguish. There are the logistical aspects of being in a period of transition. To feel all these things at once, could easily be way too much to handle at the beginning. So the mind does what it can to soften the blow. It strategically uses denial as a way for you to cope with the loss you're experiencing more easily.

After a break-up, it's normal to feel numb or to believe that life is without purpose. It's easy to feel like you've wasted your time, energy and love. And it's easy to not fully believe or accept that the break up is for real. This could be the time when certain reckless behaviors are at their peak. You might go out a lot, drink heavily, or have some meaningless sexual encounters; all the while telling yourself (and believing) that none of it matters anymore. You might spend more money than you should or make a few irrational decisions during this time. When we're feeling low, the chaotic nature of life is all too apparent. We might start wondering why we're even on this earth. We might feel like nothing really matters anymore.

These thought patterns and this numbness, as difficult as they may be to cope with at the time, could actually be denial attempting to take the sting out of what you're feeling. Because what you will notice is that when denial begins to wane, you will start *feeling* again. Numbness will give way to pain. Reality will set in. And although this can feel pretty rotten, it's actually a positive progression. When the pain starts to set in and we no longer use denial to protect ourselves from it, we are nearing the end of stage 1. We're getting a little bit closer to feeling better.

### Stage 2: Anger

Anger is a difficult emotion to deal with. Most people think of it as an ugly emotion because at times, it can lead people to act out in harmful ways. It certainly does not feel pleasant to have anger brewing in your gut. And knowing what to do with anger and where to direct it is something a lot of people struggle with. But anger is part of our lives for a reason. It's a necessary part of life, and that's because anger is a sign of *strength*. Think about comic book super-heroes who start out weak and scrawny. When they become angry, they get physically bigger, stronger, and more capable of dealing with the problem at hand. There is a lot of truth to such simplified fiction. When we're angry, we are overcoming weakness. We are "bulking up" so that we can endure the emotional hurricane that comes with a break-up. Again, this is your mind protecting you and it's a sign that you are moving forward.

But for many people, the question is, what do you *do* with anger? Where do you put it? How do you cope with it? First of all, note that when you're angry after a break-up, you may not actually feel angry at your ex. Instead, you might become angry at friends and family when they say the wrong things about your relationship or when they make mean comments about your ex.

For instance, if you're still hurting or if you still have feelings for your ex and a sibling says something to the effect of, *"Good riddance! He wasn't right for you anyway"*, you might feel your anger switch being activated. Anger can be directed towards anyone and anything during a period of grief. Think of it as being on high alert emotionally. During the anger stage, you might find that you are more angry at other things than you are at your ex. This might be because you're feeling anger and denial at the same time. You might just not be ready to face the anger you have towards your ex yet. You may be angry at the world instead. You may be angry at yourself. All of these things are normal. The important thing with anger is that you let yourself *feel it*. That is what you *do* with anger. You have to let it run its course. So try not to stifle it. When anger bubbles up, let yourself experience it. Don't fight it. Say it out loud. Say that you're angry and that you hate this whole situation. Say whatever comes to your mind even if you have no one to say it to. The sooner you allow yourself to feel your feelings, the quicker you will get over your ex.

Remember that as you progress through the stages of grief, there may be overlaps and you may go forwards and backwards throughout the process. This is normal. It is not a sign that something is wrong with you or that it will take you any longer to recover. Go easy on yourself during these early stages. Grief isn't easy, so try to be gentle with yourself. If there are people or situations that you know are going to cause you to blow, consider avoiding those triggers for a while. Letting yourself feel anger does not mean letting yourself go on a rampage. This doesn't mean that you should avoid facing your feelings, but rather it might be a way to keep the other relationships in your life on stable ground during this acute stage.

## Stage 3: Bargaining

Bargaining is when your mind tries to do everything it can to turn back time. This is often the stage where people decide to go back to their ex in the hope of getting back together. It's the time when you might start thinking that you were the one at fault and that if you'd only done things differently, everything would've been fine. Again, you might find a hint of denial still lingering when you get to stage 3. The mind wants so badly for the pain to end, so it tries to convince you that you shouldn't have broken up in the first place. *Things weren't really that bad. If you do things differently this time, it'll all work out.* So maybe you start bargaining with what you have to offer. You think about what went wrong and how *you* could change to make it all better. Maybe you could make more time for your ex the second time around. Maybe you could be more supportive, less bitchy, whatever it was that got in the way in the first place. You might decide that actually, you *can* put up with your ex's faults and flaws. You can forgive them.

During this stage, you may also start to struggle with feelings of guilt. You might conveniently forget about the part your ex played in the break-up. You might start blaming yourself and wishing you'd been a better partner. During this time, you might form some plans to make things better. You might reach out to your ex even though you know you probably shouldn't. This might be the time when your friends' advice gets tossed to the side and you forge ahead in a potentially misguided attempt to build a friendship with your ex. Maybe if you could at least remain friends, this wouldn't hurt so bad.

Again, all of these thoughts and behaviors are normal. Similarly, many people in the bargaining stage will consider going back to an ex that they dated before their current ex. They bargain themselves into believing that *that* relationship was the one they should've stuck with. Maybe they should give that one a second try. But be mindful of thought patterns like this and try to remind yourself that those thoughts are not coming from a logical mind. They are simply a symptom of grief.

When it comes to coping with the bargaining stage, try to imagine that it was a friend who was in the situation instead of you. How would you advise someone if they were in your shoes? What encouragement would you offer them? What warnings would you give them? This is what you have to do for yourself when your mind tries to bargain you back into a broken relationship. Listen to that advice from within. Try to give yourself the encouragement to carry on. Try to keep your head on straight and think logically instead of emotionally.

Remind yourself of why you broke up. Remind yourself of the things in your relationship that were not fixable. Remind yourself that if you go back there, you are likely to get hurt all over again. If you slip up and send your ex a text, forgive yourself and move on. These things happen. Do your best to not get pulled back into that drama and pain. Step back and try to get refocused again. Emotions are powerful things. They can make us do things that we know aren't good for ourselves. So don't beat yourself up if you take a few steps back. Just do your best to regroup and rebuild the boundaries you need to keep yourself safe from a relationship that is now in your past.

**Stage 4: Depression**
Stage 4 is perhaps the most expected part of grief. It is also the stage that is most commonly associated with break-ups. In a film, a person in stage 4 might be shown looking disheveled, lonely, eating a tub of ice cream and crying over a sappy movie. But depression usually isn't that easy, nor that steeped in cliche. Being depressed can feel like you're crumbling beneath the weight of your emotions. It can feel like you can't go on and that your pain will last forever.

You might sleep a lot or you might not be able to sleep at all. You might cry at things you normally wouldn't cry about. When someone at work asks you if you're okay, you might struggle to swallow the lump in your throat. Your concentration and productivity may suffer. You might feel inclined to batten down the hatches, stay in the house and be alone rather than having to face the world. You might not want to talk to your friends and family. You might not want to do anything at all. Your appetite may come and go. If you have experienced clinical depression in the past, your period of depression may be even worse, or it may last longer. This is the part of breaking up when reality sets in, and that is why it can feel so bad. Denial and anger have passed by this stage. You know now that the break-up is real, that there is no going back. And that hurts.

Thinking about the future may be impossible while you are at this stage, and that's okay. When you're depressed, it's important that you take good care of yourself. Don't beat yourself up for it. Don't force yourself to look forward to the future if you're not ready to. But do everything you can to *actively cope* with it. This means doing your best to not let it consume you. And the way you can do that isn't by trying to ignore it or fighting it, it's by putting a few practical measures in place. Eat well and try to get a little bit of exercise every day. Don't cancel plans with your friends, or hideaway. Being social, as difficult as it may be during this time, is a fantastic weapon against depression. The more you keep living your life as you normally would, the sooner depression will leave you. Do your very best to avoid alcohol and recreational drugs during this time. Some substances are very good at *maintaining* depression and that's not what you want. In addition, the more you numb the pain, the longer it may hang around.

Like anger, the feelings related to depression just want to be felt. Yes, it hurts. Yes, you will cry. Yes, you may go through stages 1 to 3 all over again during this time. It's not easy, but all of this is normal. The important thing to remember about depression is that it will end. No matter who you are or what else you are going through right now, depression is never permanent. It is a temporary state that will pass. Remind yourself of this when you're at your lowest. Try to reach out to a friend or family member so you can get things off your chest. Most importantly, if you are considering harming yourself in any way, or if you feel as though you cannot cope, seek professional help immediately.

Getting help is nothing to feel ashamed of, we all need it sometimes. If you're feeling like you shouldn't be alone right now, don't be. Have a friend come to stay with you or go stay with a family member if possible. Get out of the house if you need to. Go to the movies, sit at a diner and drink coffee, be around people. Take the best possible care of yourself that you can during this stage and keep reminding yourself that it will end soon. You're almost at the end of the grieving process now, so hang in there. Remember that some things have to get worse before they get better, but this is the end of the line for break-up pain. You **will** get through this.

## Stage 5: Acceptance

No matter how long it takes you to get to this point, there will come a day when you open your eyes in the morning and notice that you feel a little bit lighter. It will most likely be a gradual change, you might not even notice it happening at the start. Acceptance can sneak up on you, and when it does, it's a welcome surprise. So what does acceptance look like? Well, it probably won't be as miraculous as it sounds. You're not likely to wake up and spontaneously love the idea of being out of the relationship; at least not for a while. But you might finally feel like you've gotten used to the idea of it. Your pain may not be completely gone, but you might start to look forward to your future again. **Acceptance means that you have learned to live with things as they are.**

The idea of *"moving on"* might start to seem more realistic, whatever that looks like for you. Maybe you'll be ready to start meeting new people, or maybe you'll decide to try being on your own for a while. Maybe you'll feel more motivated to do something new or to put more energy into your work or your passion. Maybe you'll start feeling less out of place when you're out socializing, or more able to let go and have a good time. You might notice that you're crying less and that you have more hours feeling good than bad. These are all signs that you have at least started to adjust to the change and that you are getting over the loss.

In the future, as you move further and further away from your break-up, you may still have moments where you feel sentimental or sad about how things went down. Reflecting back on your relationship might still cause you to feel some pain. But with time, you will continue to heal. As you move forward, you will notice that you think about and talk about your ex less and less. You will have new things to talk about. Your new life will start to feel more exciting and independent. And it is around this time that you really need to give yourself credit for getting through the grieving process. You should feel proud that you have overcome your pain. Most importantly, you can be excited about your future. You have braved the worst of it.

# How To Cope With Your Emotions

Throughout your break-up, you will, unfortunately, have to cope with some really difficult emotions. As you progress through the grieving period, it's only natural that your mind will wander onto subjects that are hard to handle. If you were not the one who initiated the break-up, you may feel overwhelmed by the feelings attached to rejection. So too, if you broke up with someone who did not accept you for who you are, or who bullied or abused you in any way, rejection will be something that you'll have to face. Coping with rejection isn't easy, especially when it comes from someone we care about or from someone who knows us well. It's only natural to feel wounded at times like these. But in times of rejection, there are things you can do to make things easier on yourself. Rejection is the opposite of approval, so consider some ways you can increase your feelings of being approved of in order to balance out the feelings of rejection you're experiencing.

Spend time with people who know and love you. Be around your friends and close family members. Try not to give in to negative thought patterns like, "my ex was the only one who really knew me" or *"I have no one else in my life that really cares about me"*, etc. You have to be able to let go of the person who is no longer there and cling to those who are. Remember that if people didn't think highly of you, they wouldn't want to be around you. So take solace in the fact that the people are there supporting you, the ones who are texting to check up on you and taking you out for the night, are there because they approve of you. Those are the people to surround yourself with at this time. Try to avoid being around anyone who actively rejects or criticizes you a lot. They might not be the best company while you're feeling fragile. If you do have to be around people who aren't the kindest, keep your cards close to your chest in order to protect yourself from them.

Furthermore, when it comes to approval and rejection, the best medicine is that which lies within. Throughout the course of our lives, all of us have to be able to approve of ourselves. This is something that will serve you well for the rest of your life. The more we focus on approving of ourselves, the easier it is to cope with moments of failure and rejection. Take a few minutes now and write a list of things that you love about yourself. Then write another list of things that you're good at. And finally, write a third list of things that you have accomplished so far in life. I promise you this will be time well spent, so try not to skip it. Exercises like this take very little time and energy while offering big rewards. They're a great way to change your outlook and remind you of all the positive things in your life. They help you recognize how strong you are and how much positivity you still have left in your life. When it comes to approving of yourself, exercises like this will help you get a grasp on all the things you have to offer. It can be hard to focus on our strengths when we're in a period of weakness. So no matter how silly you feel doing it, get a pen and paper now and give yourself 10 minutes to do this exercise.

For each of the three lists, write down between 5 and 10 things. Do not let yourself get away with writing down less than 5. Once you have written down at least 15 positive things about yourself and your life, let yourself feel good about those things. Feel released from all the negativity that's around you right now. Feel good about your potential for the future. And feel proud of all that you have overcome thus far in life.

After a break-up, one of the hardest things to get your head around is what your future will be like. There are a lot of unknowns in life, and around this time, you will probably be facing quite a few of them. The things that we can't predict can be the hardest things to cope with. No one likes to feel out of control or unsure about what direction their life is going in. If this is something you're experiencing now, it's natural to feel bitter or to feel resentment towards your ex. These are complicated emotions and if they're not handled delicately, they can lead to a deeper sense of unhappiness or cynicism. It is true that having to adjust to a major change can be disorienting. If you have gone from a place of security and comfort to a place of uncertainty and chaos, it is natural to resent your ex. But it's important that you don't let these feelings take root!

Too much bitterness could bring out the worst in you and prevent you from trusting people in the future, and that's something that you might want to avoid. Remember that it's okay to feel your feelings. It's important that you listen to your heart and give yourself time to grieve. Just keep an eye out for any signs of lingering bitterness. When bitterness is allowed to run rampant, it can distort reality and change who you are at the core. But there is an antidote to bitterness, and that is positivity. So tell yourself that this break-up is not strong enough to break you. Hold onto any positivity you can get a grip on during this time. Soak up the positive in every situation and repel the negative. Spend time with people you like, and limit time around people you don't like. Spend time doing things that you enjoy, and limit time spent doing things you don't enjoy. Do everything you can to balance out your negativity with positivity.

There will be times when the negativity wins for the day, and that's okay. You can try again tomorrow. The best thing you can do is to actively listen to your feelings and respond accordingly. If you're sad, do something that will comfort you. If you're feeling negatively charged, do something that will relax and rejuvenate you. If you're feeling numb or hopeless, seek someone or something that inspires you. Play an active part in your feelings.

Finally, if you have been cheated on or betrayed, take extra care with yourself. When someone cheats on their partner, it can cause some of the most intense feelings of rejection there are. Feeling as though you aren't good enough or as if you have been cast aside is not pleasant. Being deceived is a terrible thing to have to go through. It can be unbelievably painful and very difficult to express, especially when it comes from the person you trust the most. You may react with anger but inside you may feel completely crushed. You may be worried that you'll never be able to trust anyone again. You may feel like if you're not good enough for your ex, you're not good enough for anyone. But none of that is true. When someone cheats, they are doing so because of something that is wrong within them, not something that is wrong with their partner. For whatever reason, if your ex cheated on you, they did so because they were cowardly. They did not have enough guts to do the right thing. That is a flaw within them, not within you. Many times, when someone is unhappy in a relationship but they're too weak to face that reality, they go into self-destruct mode. That might mean that they get drunk and make mistakes. It might mean that they cheat or lie. It may mean that they spend extravagant amounts of money or disrespect you in public.

**None of these things are your fault.** These are problems that your ex will have to face in their own time. And if this is the case in your break-up, do everything you can to distance yourself from that person and focus on you. There is no use in trying to help someone who has disrespected or deceived you. You cannot help someone who clearly needs to learn to help themself. You do not have to forgive them either. Remind yourself that your ex did not cheat on you because you weren't good enough. No matter what negative thought patterns are running through your mind, you have to fight them. You have to tell yourself that you are good enough. You have to try to approve of yourself. Yes, you will need time to heal. And some of this pain could take a long time to get over. You may develop some relationship phobias as a result of it. But if you're actively doing what you can to cancel out that negativity, you will recover. Be good to yourself during this time. Treat yourself with respect and care. Do nice things for yourself. And do everything you can to steer clear of anyone who has treated you wrongly.

# Protecting Yourself 101

Human beings require a sense of safety and security throughout their lives, no matter how old we are, how much money we make, or how self-sufficient we are. We need to balance out the chaos in the world around us. We need to be able to make sense of the goings on in our lives, to feel supported in our endeavors, and to simply know that we're not alone. One of the most common ways we can achieve that safety and security is through our relationships with others. This includes family members, friends, and of course, lovers and intimate partners. Even when someone is in a relationship that is tumultuous or problematic, even if they are often hurt by their loved one, they may still satisfy that need for safety and security through that relationship. In life, structure can make all the difference, even if it's not built solely on positive grounds. Unfortunately, when the structure of a relationship changes, it can have a massive effect on you and your life. It can distort your sense of safety and security, leaving you in a period of dizzying change. When a relationship ends, not only are you forced to grieve that loss, but you are also forced to find new ways to achieve the sense of safety and security that we all need. The problem is knowing what to do and how to emotionally protect yourself when facing such monumental change.

One of the most common and harmful ways people cope with situations like these is to attempt to get that safety and security back from their ex. Rebuilding your life is hard, especially when you're hurting. But if you continue to focus on your ex as the keeper of your security, you will be prolonging your grieving time and making things a lot harder for yourself than they need to be. And I'm not just talking about trying to get back together with your ex. I'm talking about stalking them online or in person. I'm talking about texting and calling your ex. I'm talking about attending events in the hopes that your ex will be there. And above all, I'm talking about relying on your ex for approval, support, or even reaching out to them to help you get through your break-up pain *(trust me, this is something that plenty of people do)*.

It is natural to feel disappointed, disheartened, and even hopeless when you're forced to face your future alone. It is normal to feel scared, to be angry, and to wish you had better success with relationships. Being alone will take some time to adjust to; unfortunately, time is always an element when it comes to healing emotionally. But if you learn how to protect yourself and you dedicate yourself to doing so, your difficult times will come to an end much sooner and far more easily. Remember that you aren't just coping with a break-up, you're also facing a new chapter in your life. You can embrace the positivity in that change by focusing on yourself and looking forward, or you can fight that change by holding onto something that has already sadly passed.

So how does one protect one's self and start walking forward into the future when they are still haunted by the pain in their past? Put simply, the more you limit contact with your ex, the quicker you will recover. Have a look at the following list which briefly describes the rules of disengagement. Note that I have mentioned the need for getting space a few times already in this book and there is a good reason for that. Try to keep an open mind as you read through this list and remember that it's natural to feel upset when thinking about these things. Remember to treat yourself kindly as you take this information on board. Take a break whenever you need to. Do something nice for yourself or do something that you find relaxing. The aim is to stop focusing on your ex and start focusing on yourself.

# The 4 Rules of Disengagement and How To Stick To Them

## 1.) Limit contact or cut it off completely.

I have mentioned this previously, and I know it may sound harsh, but as you know, if you stay in contact with your ex during your grieving period, you are only going to hurt yourself and stall your recovery. If you text them when you're drunk, you will probably regret it. If you talk to them on the phone, you will only feel increased yearning and sadness. Contact with exes is a minefield. Not only are you reminding yourself of your loss, but you are also opening yourself up to more potential pain.

What if you're talking to your ex and they seem to be getting over things a lot faster than you are?
How will that feel if you still feel buried beneath the weight of it and they seem to be fine?
What will it feel like to hear that they're rebounding or dating other people already?

Exposing yourself to potential jealousy can make you feel a lot worse than you already do.
What will it feel like if they tell you that they're struggling with the break-up or that they regret how things have gone?
How can you focus on your own healing if you're still carrying your ex around, emotionally speaking?

There are endless possibilities when it comes to this type of hypothetical questioning, the vast majority of which will have negative outcomes.

It is never easy to walk away from someone you once loved or continue to love. Our partners are our best friends. They're our family. Separating from them will hurt. You may feel like you're incomplete for a while. You might be worried about what your future will be like. You might not think that you can endure life without them. But I promise you that you can and you will. Furthermore, remember that you might be able to get back in contact with your ex when the dust settles. This doesn't have to be a permanent measure. Take a moment now to think about other losses that you have lived through. Were they easy to cope with? Probably not. But you made it. You got through it. You were strong enough then, and you are still strong enough now. No matter how hard it was, you survived, and you will do again.

Human beings are unbelievably resilient. We have an immense ability to cope when things go wrong. Take solace in that, even when it feels like you're not coping well. Believe that you have the power to come through this thing on your own. You do not need to cling to something that is over now. Yes, it is hard to let go. Unbelievably hard. But if you cut off contact with the source of your pain, your heart will be allowed to un-break itself. Talking to your ex will only remind you of the pain. It will hold you back from moving on. It will keep you rooted to the spot. You deserve to focus on you right now.

So, at least for the time being, take a break from communicating with your ex. If you need to get in touch with them to organize things like children or swapping belongings, keep your communication brief and direct. Don't give in to the inclination to talk about your emotions or listen to them talk about theirs. Set a boundary where those things are concerned. You both need space and time to heal. Maybe you will be able to reconnect in the future on a friendly basis, but for now, you need to take a break from each other.

**2.) Stay safe online.**
Life online has added a whole new level to relationships and break-ups. Remaining connected to an ex online is a broken heart waiting to happen. The temptation to look at your ex's status updates can be excruciating. When you're lonely, you might want to look them up and see what they're up to. But this is extremely dangerous behavior, emotionally speaking. Looking at your ex will only remind you that you're no longer together. If they are out socializing and appearing like they're on top of the world, that isn't going to feel good. If you see them online and it looks like they're an emotional wreck, you're going to feel inclined to help them or feel guilty. None of these things are good options when you're trying to focus on yourself. And

don't forget about paranoia. It's easy to become obsessed if someone new starts commenting on your ex's status updates. It's easy to become overly fixated on any new friends they may have made since the break-up.

You could easily drive yourself crazy with stuff like that; wondering who they are and what's going on between the two of them, when in fact there mightn't be anything to it at all. So if you want to stay safe online, start by deleting, blocking, or at least limiting what posts you see from your ex. Resist online stalking, checking up on them, or checking their friends' pages for indicators of their current status. Do not ask your friends to check up on them if they have blocked you. When the temptation strikes, step away from the computer.

Think about what you are like and what behaviors will be the hardest to crack for you. Then set rules for yourself accordingly. Do you often check social media after you've had a few drinks? If so, set a rule for yourself about it and eliminate that behavior, stat. You can always come back to social media when the dust has settled and you're sober. Give your phone to a friend if you're out together, switch off all your devices at a specific time each night, delete your social media pages from your mobile phone so that they're not with you all the time. Do whatever you have to do to get away from social media for a while if it's something that you know is a trigger for you. This is a strong measure of self-protection and preservation. You will never regret taking a step back from life online for a while. It can be liberating to take that time for yourself.

The thing is, social media is great and fun when things in your life are going well. But when life seems like it's crashing down all around you, it can feel like an invasive, maddening, negative force. When you're feeling low, life online can make you paranoid. It can give you a window into something that you don't necessarily need to see. The temptation to check up on your ex may be really intense at times, but if you want to hurt less, you have to limit your exposure to them. Be strong in your resolve. Ask your friends to support you through this. If you can text a friend rather than stalking your ex online, do it. When you're feeling low, challenge yourself to put your phone and other devices away so that you don't have to live through that temptation. Remember that the aim of the game is to make things easier for you. This is not a punishment. The future is still wide open, and there will come a day when looking at your ex online will no longer trigger you. But until then, step back and switch off.

### 3.) Do not rely on your ex for anything.

One of the hardest things about breaking-up is figuring out all the logistical stuff. This is especially true if you were living together or if you shared a lot of responsibilities between the two of you. Having to do everything by yourself isn't easy for anyone, and if you've broken up with someone who was helpful in regards to getting things done, it's going to be even harder. The simple matter of time will likely affect you in a way it hadn't done before.

How will you manage to do all the laundry and the grocery shopping on your own while juggling your work schedule?

How will you make sure the dog gets walked, the DIY jobs get finished, and dinner is cooked when you're already swamped?

These are valid concerns for anyone who isn't used to doing *everything* by themselves. And unfortunately, in addition to the emotional mess you're dealing with, these are also things you will need to think about and plan for. It's not ideal, it may take some trial and error, and it could cause you some short-term stress. But the important thing is that you don't remain tied to your ex by asking them to help out. This is not only because of the emotional difficulties and extended period of grieving that you might end up having as a result of continued contact, but it will also hold you back from gaining the sense of independence that you need right now. The more we rely on our exes, the more we are telling ourselves that we can't live without them. We are telling ourselves that we are not complete, that we are not competent, and that we can't be self-sufficient. These are all potentially harmful thought patterns when what you need is to feel confident and empowered.

So take some time, as soon as you can, to start making plans and arrangements that do not involve relying on your ex for help. Unless a task has to do with your children or another mutually owned responsibility, you can do this on your own. Think about asking close friends or family members to give you a hand for a while if you're struggling to keep on top of everything. You might just need someone to help temporarily until you figure out how you can manage it all on your own. After a break-up, the people who care about you will probably be happy to help, so don't hesitate to reach out to them. It is possible that you might need to make some big changes to your life as well as some minor adjustments.

If you have to find a new place to live or something else that's of a similar magnitude, you will probably experience an increase to your stress levels. This might cause you to feel resentment toward your ex or you may experience a rise in anger and sadness. These are all normal responses, so make sure that you treat yourself kindly during this time. Get as much help as you can from other people in your life and try not to worry about the little things when there are more pressing matters at hand. Don't sweat the little stuff. You might have a hard time keeping up with things like cleaning the house while coping with an increasingly busy schedule, but to minimize the impact of heightened stress levels on your self-esteem, try to let go of those insignificant things. If the house needs to be a mess for a while so that you can catch up with everything else, that's okay. Try not to let it upset you or bother you too much.

The important thing is that you're taking good care of yourself while rejigging and reorganizing your responsibilities. Make sure that you prioritize self-care. Make sure that you're eating right and getting plenty of rest. Juggling the emotional stuff alongside the logistical stuff can be overwhelming, so do everything you can to make things easier on yourself without reaching out to your ex. Use the other people in your life for help, take some time off work if you need to, move your schedule around to make things more manageable, and let go of the little things for now. Eventually, things will even out again, and you'll be surprised to find just how self-sufficient you can be. In the meantime, try to take things one day at a time and resist the urge to call your ex for help at all costs.

**4.) Stay safe when you're out and about.**

Even if we haven't experienced it for ourselves, we can all imagine what it's like to run into an ex when you're not expecting it. The potential for sadness, jealousy, and awkward encounters is ripe for the taking when something like this happens. Moreover, if you think it's a good idea to attend an event that you know your ex is also planning on attending, you might be being a little naive. Even if you ended the relationship on good terms, seeing and being around your ex won't help you in your journey to an independent future. That is why I keep repeating this sentiment. Yes, there may be times when seeing your ex is unavoidable. And with plenty of preparation, you should be able to survive those things that are genuinely unavoidable. But if you can avoid seeing your ex when you're out, you should.

This may mean missing events that you were looking forward to. It may mean not going to certain bars and restaurants for a while. It may mean not getting to hang out with your friends as much if your ex is also friends with them. None of these things are ideal, and sometimes it can feel like you've lost the free will to go out and socialize as you please. But think of this as a temporary measure. You don't necessarily have to avoid your ex forever, just consider waiting for the dust to settle first.

Remember that when you've lost your sense of security and safety, your mind could be subconsciously telling you to do anything in your power to get that back. For this reason, you may feel inclined to drive by your ex's house or their workplace to catch a glimpse of them. You might consider going to events just because you think your ex might be there. You might tell yourself over and over that it'll be fine if you run into them and that you're not going to change your plans just because you're afraid of seeing them.

These inclinations are all relatively common. Many people do have a hard time staying away from a person when their mind is fully focused them. But again, continuing to go back to a source of pain is like emotional self-harm. No matter what you see, it's going to hurt. It will hurt if you see your ex with someone new. It will hurt if you see them looking lonely. It will hurt regardless of any circumstance they're in. Have you ever heard of someone seeking out a glimpse of their ex and coming back feeling good? Probably not. It is true that the mind is fragile, and when we're heavily focused on another person, we can get a little carried away from time to time. But the more you resist the urge to see your ex, and the more you can truly focus on *you*, the better you will feel and the sooner you will get over this.

It is natural to feel like you're at a loose end if your safety and security have been obliterated. It's natural to want to regain that connection, even when it hurts and you know it's not going to help. But try to do your best to protect yourself from added pain. You deserve that much. Try to focus on yourself. Try out some new bars and restaurants. Make plans with friends that you haven't seen in a while. Change any plans you already have if you know your ex is going to be in the same place. If you do have to attend an event where you know your ex will be, try to get a friend to come with you and avoid sitting near or talking to your ex. If you're starting to feel emotionally activated because of their presence, leave the environment and do something relaxing instead. Ask a friend to hang out with you until you feel better. Avoid the temptation to drink heavily or have a spontaneous confrontation with your ex. It can feel terrible having to make these decisions, especially if you're not emotionally ready to let go. But if you can reduce your exposure to potentially painful run-ins, it will help. Think of this as the beginning of gaining your own safety and security.

## Breakup Case Story: Robbie

*When my partner Josh and I split up, the loss completely consumed me. We'd met in college, and neither of us had ever been in a serious relationship before. We came from similar backgrounds. Both of us went to high schools where it was not exactly cool to be gay, so finding each other in college was really special. At first, we kept things casual, but it wasn't long before we were a real couple. It was an exciting time. The thing about Josh was that he really seemed to get me in a way that no one else ever had. He loved me even when I didn't I love myself. He knew how to talk to me when I was being overly emotional, and he indulged my need for him to say "I love you" at least twice a day.*

*As the years passed, things changed. We still really cared about each other, and we were best friends, but the spark had died. It was awful when we made the decision to part ways, but it was for the best. We decided to stay friends, but it was really hard at first. I hated being around him with this wall between us. I didn't adjust well to the new boundaries of friendship. I lived in constant fear that he might tell me he'd found someone new. I just couldn't bear the thought of it. I wasn't ready to move on, but he was. The thought of it haunted me. What I realized was that I needed to get some distance from him so I could have a chance to heal. It wasn't easy telling Josh that I needed him to stop texting me for a while. We still saw each other pretty often after the break-up. We were still going to the same events together and hanging out with our shared group of friends. Not much had changed. But it was killing me inside. So I told him that I needed to get some space from him but that we could be friends when I was feeling solid again.*

*The time we spent apart was excruciating at times. Josh wasn't just my ex; he was also my best friend. I wasn't sure who I could talk to about my feelings when he was the person I felt the safest with. But I stuck to my guns. I hung out with our friends when I knew he wouldn't be around. I stopped texting him despite how tough it was. And after a while, I started to heal. I guess one day I just woke up feeling lighter. I knew that my relationship with Josh wasn't a failure. It was wonderful while it lasted and I learned so much about myself and the world when I was with him. Now, we're best friends again. We both have new boyfriends, and we're both happy. I can still lean on him when I need support, but it doesn't hurt anymore knowing that we're just friends. What we needed to get where we are today, was as simple as taking some time apart. I honestly believe that if I hadn't have given myself the time away from him and gotten back on my own two feet, I would've felt attached to him forever. I never would've been able to be friends with him if I hadn't taken the time to mourn. In the end, our break-up did not break us, and I'm so thankful for that.*

# The Truth About Rebounds

This book is not designed to boss you around or judge your behavior in the wake of your break-up. For this reason, it will not offer any black and white rules when it comes to rebounds. Things like this are rarely straight forward. Nothing is all good or all bad for everyone. We are all individuals, and each situation is different from the rest. So with this understanding of the human experience in mind, this section will seek to help you better understand the potential intentions behind rebounding so that you can make the best decision for yourself. Let's start by thinking about what is meant by the word *rebounding* and the reasons people may choose to do it.

Firstly, there are two types of rebounds: the sexual and the emotional. And just as human beings are complex, so are these two types of rebounds. If you're inclined to rebound, you might seek one type of rebound or the other, or you may seek a mixture of the two. Sexual rebounds often involve one night stands, 'no strings attached' sex, or arrangements like 'friends with benefits'. Emotional rebounds can be a little more complex. They may also involve a sexual element, but emotional rebounds also usually include a deeper connection as well. Emotional rebounds usually involve going on dates with someone, communicating with someone on a deeper level, being in regular contact with someone, or diving into a whole new relationship. The reasons people rebound vary from person to person, but the most common reasons include not being ready to be alone, seeking a distraction from emotional pain or difficult thoughts, wanting to blow off steam, seeking revenge, trying to fill an emotional void, or genuinely liking someone new despite the bad timing.

For some reason, despite how long our lives can be, following a break-up, things can feel incredibly urgent. This is also true during other times of heightened emotions or loss. Feeling a sense of urgency is often a symptom of being overwhelmed by your emotions. When it feels like your world has come crashing down all around you, it's hard not to get swept away in the hurricane of change. If your emotions are all-consuming, it will naturally be hard for you to get perspective. And when we don't have perspective, our behavior can become a little erratic or irresponsible. These are all normal reactions to major periods of transition. So too, when we experience a loss, it is natural to try to fill that void.

Don't forget how our innate need for safety and security can kick into high gear after a break-up. By attempting to satisfy that need, perhaps we won't feel it so badly. Maybe if we fill that void right away, everything will be fine, and the pain of it will recede without us even noticing. It's natural to want some distraction if you're buried beneath the weight of a lost relationship. It is completely normal to want to blow off steam and forget your pain whenever you can. As you can see, the complexity in the inclination to rebound is astounding, and it's far from black and white.

In the interest of keeping yourself safe and recovering as quickly as possible, take some time to think about your own inclination to rebound. Of course, you may not want to rebound at all, but if you do, try to ask yourself why.
 Do you just need a distraction right now?
Do you want to go wild because you're angry about how things went down with your ex?
Do you feel unready to be alone?

Try to be honest with yourself about this, because the more you can understand your own thoughts and behaviors, the more clearly you will be thinking and the more able you will be to make good choices. The thing that you need to consider in order to stay on the right rebound path is what state your mind is in, and what type of person you are. For instance, if you know that you don't feel good after having meaningless sex, a 'no strings attached' arrangement is not going to be the best thing for you. There are plenty of people in the world who cannot emotionally cope with casual sex. It is difficult for a lot of people to not become attached to someone after they've slept with them.

A lot of this is down to hormonal responses, but regardless of the reason, if you become attached to someone who is not emotionally available, you could very easily be adding even more weight to the emotional baggage you're currently carrying. There is nothing wrong with being the type of person who cannot separate sex from emotional and intellectual attachment. The problem occurs when someone like this decides to have casual sex and ends up getting hurt. So if you are this type of person, keep yourself safe by avoiding erratic sexual behavior.

If it's a distraction that you're looking for and you are the type of person who can happily have casual sex, you may be able to do so while remaining emotionally safe. However, you must be honest with yourself about why you behave the way you do. If you are seeking a distraction, that might be fine. But if you're using casual sex as a way to ignore your feelings about the break-up, you could be prolonging your grieving time. Imagine placing a big heavy dictionary on the floor in the middle of your living room. You can look in every different direction in order to ignore that book, but no matter how good you are at averting your eyes from it, if you want to walk through the middle of the room, you're going to have to face the fact that the book is still there. You will eventually have to bend down, pick it up, put it where it belongs. This is what happens when you use rebounds as a distraction from your pain.

Yes, casual sex might actually make you feel better in some ways, and it could be a good way to get your mind off that weighty subject. But in the end, your break-up will still be there until you're prepared to face it and grieve it away. The most effective way to get through difficult emotions is to let yourself feel them. There is no substitute for feeling. And yes, some people can get really good at ignoring their feelings, but even when they do, you can bet those emotions are still locked inside them somewhere. So, if you are the type of person who feels comfortable with sexual rebounding, by all means do what you need to do in order to blow off steam and have a good time, just as long as you get real with yourself about your true emotions and you let yourself process them. Keep your wits about you. Who cares what things are like on the surface if you're being eaten away inside?

Another important facet of rebounding that you might want to think about is getting trapped in cyclical patterns of Internet dating.

Because the nature of dating has changed so much in the last decade, it is easy to become addicted to online dating and end up feeling depressed and disappointed on repeat. When your brain needs time to process the loss of one relationship, the last thing it needs is to have to cope with the rise of multiple new ones. The thing about Internet dating specifically is that it encourages people to date a number of people at once. When one person's out, the next person is there waiting to take their place. But being involved with this high turnover dating will not only hold you back from getting over your ex, but it could also leave you feeling devalued, emotionally lost, or believing that you will always be unlucky in love. This is not to say that everyone with an online dating profile has bad intentions, or that Internet dating is bad in general. But it is to say that when you are trying to get over someone, you might not find emotional peace via *Tinder*. If you're not careful with these things, you could end up getting hurt again long before you're ready to.

Again, you have to do what you think is best for you. Maybe you do need a short burst of frivolous dating to take your mind off things. But eventually, your feelings will need to be addressed. Keep in mind too, that it's not very nice to use someone else for your rebound if they're looking for something more. Make sure that whatever your intent is, it should be matched by whomever it is that you're dating. Don't let your post-break-up behavior lead you to hurt an innocent person.

Finally, if you are considering starting a serious relationship directly after your break-up, use caution. Even if you want to get involved with someone you've known for years and you know that they understand your situation, it's always a good idea to wait a little while before getting into a new relationship. When we go straight into a new relationship after a break-up, we might not be in the best place emotionally. This could mean dragging some of your pain and discontentment into your new relationship. If you were betrayed by your ex, you might not be fully ready to trust someone else yet. If you're afraid of getting hurt again, you might not be able to actually enjoy being in a new relationship. You might constantly be worried that it'll all go wrong again. Think of your break-up like a physical wound. Let's say that you've cut your finger so badly that you need stitches. Would you welcome the thought of cutting the same finger in the same place again before it's even healed? Probably not, because that sounds like agony.

The moral of the story is, be mindful of your behavior when it comes to rebounds. Be careful with your heart. Try to think about why you want to do the things you're inclined to do. Think about how you will feel as a result of a rebound, regardless of what type of rebound it is or who it's with. Most importantly, try to keep in mind that although emotional pain can be awful, the quickest and most effective way to get relief from it is to let yourself feel it so that it can pass naturally. We all need a distraction from time to time, but ignoring our feelings is never the path to freedom from them. Protect yourself the best you can if you've decided to start dating again. Have fun, but try to take things slowly. There is plenty of time ahead of you.

# Understanding Your Relationship Patterns

Going through a break-up doesn't have to be all bad. It can present us with an opportunity to make some much-needed changes in our lives, which can be the up side to the loss we've endured. Being able to better understand ourselves, our patterns, and our feelings is always a positive thing, especially when it comes to putting a stop to harmful habits. The more we understand about ourselves, the better we can make our lives and pave the way for a happier future. Our relationships with other people can tell us a lot about ourselves and why our lives are the way they are. How we relate to other people is complex, and this is not limited to intimate partners. The nature of our relationships with friends, family members, and colleagues is also of great importance when it comes to better understanding ourselves and changing harmful relationship patterns.

When a baby is born, only a few years will pass before its *relationship blueprint* is written. The way we relate to others is almost always directly related to the way we were treated by our primary caregivers in our childhood. For example, those who are born to parents that respond their needs quickly and efficiently are likely to feel a stronger sense of safety and security than a baby whose cries go unanswered. It is this first relationship in a child's life that lays out the blueprint for most relationships they will have throughout their childhood, adolescence, and into their adulthood. For a small child whose primary caregiver is always available, their sense of personal security and safety is likely to lead to a lifetime of similarly loving, caring, secure relationships. They are likely to have a healthy self-esteem, realistic expectations of themselves, and the ability to withstand criticism and adversity. They may be more likely to set appropriate boundaries in relationships and maintain a clear understanding of their own needs and desires. But a small child who is neglected, for instance, may struggle to obtain a similar sense of security. If their relationship blueprint is written by a primary caregiver who does not respond to their need for love, approval, and acceptance, they may experience relationships throughout their lives wherein they have to "chase" people for their love and approval.

They may surround themselves with people who reject their ideas or withhold their approval and acceptance.

Once a person's relationship blueprint is written, it is likely that they will be able to identify patterns related to it in their adulthood. For instance, if your mother was cold towards you or neglected your emotional needs, you may notice that your friendships and intimate relationships have a similar dynamic. You may often ignore those who offer you instant respect and approval while flocking towards people who reject you or who keep you hanging (so to speak). If one or both of your parents were self-centered and did not value your thoughts and feelings, you may have a tendency to unconsciously surround yourself with other people who treat you in similarly uncaring ways.

If you take some time over the next few days to think about all the relationships in your life, you may discover patterns that you mightn't have noticed before. You may deduce that you are often the caretaker of your relationships or that you tend to surround yourself with people who have dominant personalities. You may notice that you have clear boundaries protecting you within your relationships, or you may notice that there are no boundaries in your relationships at all. If you tend to get your heart broken a lot, or if you often feel hurt and mistreated by the people in your life, it's likely that there is a pattern there that needs some tweaking. Perhaps you are too frightened of losing people to prioritize your needs. Or maybe you have a hard time ascertaining yourself. But regardless of what patterns you may uncover, don't worry, all is not lost. One of the best things about human beings is our ability to grow and change. Regardless of what your relationship blueprint looks like today, with some determination, you can rewrite it if you want to.

Taking the time to really inspect your relationship patterns means bringing more self-awareness into future relationships. It means valuing your own feelings and learning how to get the respect you deserve. If you commit yourself to making adjustments where needed, you could completely change the nature of your future relationships. This could mean having healthier, safer, more secure and lasting relationships all around. And of course, when the relationships in our lives are healthy, our overall happiness can increase infinitely.

When we know how to set appropriate boundaries and get the respect we deserve from people, our whole lives can change. This is especially important for people who often put others before themselves. On paper, there is nothing wrong with being selfless; it can truly be a beautiful quality. But there are many people who are so focused on taking care of other people and keeping them happy, that they neglect their own needs and fail to secure similar kindnesses for themselves. If you always put yourself last, you could be subconsciously sending a message to other people telling them that it's okay for them to put you last as well. For people who do struggle with extreme empathy and care-taking behaviors, the inclination to get involved with people regardless of how they treat you is a serious danger. People like this often get caught in unhealthy dating traps, fixating on caring for other people regardless of how they are treated in return. If you notice that you often make excuses for people when their behavior towards you is unkind, this might be something you need to think about changing. If you constantly expect the best out of people and give them the benefit of the doubt no matter what, you could be actively blinding yourself to more sinister truths.

The fact is, there are a lot of people in the world who flock towards caretakers, and that's because they know they can get away with murder and that person will always be there for them. Even if they don't consciously mean to, someone could easily take advantage of your generous nature until they get all they need from you and then move on to the next person. I'm focusing on this particular personality type because it is one of the most common problems in relationship patterns. Moreover, if you are constantly focused on someone else's needs, and you fail to recognize when someone is taking advantage of you, you will have to put a good bit of work into learning to recognize what you need to change in order to get what you need out of future relationships.

One of the reasons so many people focus heavily on the other person in their relationship is that they are afraid that if they assert their needs or oppose the natural order of things, the relationship won't last. One might put up with their partner's bad behavior because they are scared that if they set appropriate boundaries, assert their own feelings about the situation, or focus on themselves at all, their partner will leave them. This fear of rejection is dangerous because the longer we remain in relationships with this dynamic, the more broken relationships we will have in the future and the harder we will have to work to get out of this cycle. When the fear of losing a partner becomes greater than the desire to stay with them, the relationship has entered a potentially harmful state. Similarly, if you tend to focus more of your energy on understanding other people's behavior and fixing other people's problems, there is often an underlying fear and refusal to focus on your own feelings and find out what's really going on for *you*. This is extremely common because let's be honest when our own thoughts and feelings are particularly difficult and dark, it's natural to want to focus on anything and anyone else than facing that. However, if this is something that you think might be relevant to you, that could be a good indicator that it's time for a change.

The important thing to know is that regardless of what your relationship patterns are, they are fixable. So regardless of if you've gone through a lot of break-ups in your life or if you're closer to the beginning of your journey, there is hope for us all. The important thing at this stage is to try to give yourself a break from dating while you're working these things out. Giving yourself time to be alone is crucial to writing new, positive habits. This is especially important if you have been in back-to-back relationships for a long time or if you just haven't been alone for a while. When we let ourselves be single, we are allowing ourselves to regain a sense of autonomy. We are building confidence, even if it feels like we're not. Learning to be alone is just as important as learning how to have healthier relationships. This is because when we're alone for a stretch of time, we start to feel more independent. We start to recognize what it is that we really need and want out of a relationship. We can hear ourselves think. We can find out who we really are. And that's a very exciting prospect. A lot of times by rushing into the next relationship too quickly, what we are actually doing is frantically trying to replace the security and safety we had when we were coupled up. But doing this means denying yourself the ability to find that safety and security within yourself.

This means that you'll be going into a new relationship while still enduring the emotional hangover of your last one. It means that you won't have the time to actively reflect on your own needs, therefore, figuring out how you can make a more fulfilling life for yourself. So, if your relationship patterns are in need of some tweaking, do your best to avoid new relationships for a while so as to fully dedicate this time to yourself and bettering your future.

Start by reflecting on all the relationships in your life and how they make you feel. Take into account your relationships with your parents and siblings. These are your oldest relationships so they could be the best ones to learn from. What was it like for you growing up? Were you well cared for? Were you bullied or neglected at home? Did you feel respected? Were you the family caretaker? Were you the clown in the family? Did you have too much or too little responsibility? Now think about how your friends and colleagues treat you and think back over other intimate relationships you've had that didn't work out. Take time as often as possible to think about how you are affected by other people and how you seem to affect them. Look for any patterns in your relationships. Look for any similarities between the relationship you had with your primary caregiver as a child and the relationships you've had in your adulthood. The similarities might not be obvious at first, so you might need to think about this more over time. Similarly, you may be able to recognize similarities, but you may struggle to find the reason behind them. This is a complex journey of understanding, so it will take some time to develop a clear theory.

Remember that this is something you can continue to reflect on throughout your life so that you can better understand yourself and how you exist in the world around you. We can always make improvements to our lives when we know why they are the way they are. Think about any flaws in your relationships that you have seen repeated again and again.

- Is there something that always goes wrong for you?

- Do you always focus on the other person in your relationships?
- Do you focus too heavily on yourself?
- Are you emotionally guarded?
- Do you flock towards people who are emotionally unavailable?
- Do you often make excuses for the way other people treat you?
- Do you blame yourself?
- Do you always blame other people?
- Would you say that you often pick the wrong people to get close to? In what ways and why?

Thinking this way and being honest with yourself will always have a positive outcome, even if it stings a little bit at first. Thinking about the past can be emotionally activating so if you do feel saddened by these things, take it slowly and make sure to allow yourself to feel your feelings. If you have a hard time being honest with yourself, imagine that your best friend was answering these questions for you. How would they describe your relationship history? What would they say that you need to work on?

Self-reflection is the first step in self-progression. The more honest we are with ourselves, the more easily we can get to the root of the problem and build the life we want for ourselves. The things that we endured in our early lives are a fantastic resource when we're trying to understand our life in the present. This is not to say that you necessarily have to relive your childhood traumas, but rather it is to say that if you think about them critically, you could uncover some very helpful meaning behind the things you struggle with. As soon as we know where things went wrong and why, then we can start to rebuild a happier and healthier life. Furthermore, if you devote yourself to learning from your own mistakes, you can be sure that you won't repeat them later and that's something you can feel great about. Think about your close friends and family as good resources for change. If you know that you often make excuses for other people, ask your friends to tell you when you're doing that so that they can help you curb that behavior. Ask them what things they have seen in your relationships that they've found worrying but may not have told you before. Just be aware that conversations like these could flag up some things that you're not ready to face yet. Make sure that the people you talk to about these things will respect your wishes if that is the case. Progression like this can work better in baby steps.

The important thing is that you dedicate yourself to this positive change and that you remain firm and honest with yourself as you move towards building better habits and relationship awareness. Remember that this process should not be used as an excuse to beat yourself up, so avoid making sweeping statements that will counteract your intention. No one is always *bad* at relationships. Anyone can make a positive change in their lives. No one is hopeless or helpless. No one should feel forced to give up on love. We can all benefit from taking time to focus on ourselves. We all need to take better care of ourselves from time to time. So as you move forward with your self-progression, remember to treat yourself kindly. Be proud of the steps you're taking toward a happier future. Reward yourself when you put a lot of work into understanding yourself better. Reward yourself when you recognize harmful patterns. Forgive yourself if you have setbacks. We all make mistakes; they are not a sign of weakness or inability. If you have a hard time changing certain patterns and behaviors, don't worry too much about it. **Just keep trying.**

Rewriting your relationship blueprint isn't easy. It takes perseverance, persistence, and practice. But the rewards at the end of a journey like this are truly incredible. Being able to recognize what you deserve and what you need in relationships means that you will be able to set appropriate boundaries. It means that you will be able to prioritize yourself as much as your future partners, and that you will surround yourself with people who respect and love you in ways that are *truly* safe and secure.

Remember that when we focus all of our attention on our partner or our ex, we are telling ourselves that we are not worthy of the same amount of love. We are not giving ourselves as much as we could be. We are holding ourselves back from finding the relationship we really deserve. As you progress through this book and long after you've finished it, keep checking in with yourself periodically. Keep thinking about and valuing your own needs. No matter what happened in your past, your future is ripe for the taking. The more effort you put into understanding yourself, the better all of your relationships will be.

## Breakup Case Study: Scott

*When Nadia left me, I was left speechless and more confused than I've ever been in my life. We'd gotten married the previous year. It was fast, we'd only been together for a year at the time, and I can't say I wasn't warned. My family and friends all told me I was jumping the gun. Give it some time. What's the rush? All the usual stuff. But I was swept away. I'd found the woman of my dreams and I was going to make her the happiest woman alive. Those two years were bliss. I know that may sound sappy but they really were the best two years of my life. Nadia was everything I hoped for and more. She was funny, smart and talented. She was the type of woman that people want to be around and I was so proud to have her by my side.*

*I honestly cannot tell you what went wrong in our relationship because it still makes no sense to me. We were trying to get pregnant. The romance was alive and kicking. We'd gotten a puppy after our decadent honeymoon in the Caribbean. We were happy. It was a few weeks after our first wedding anniversary when my whole world went up in smoke. On Saturday night, we went to our favorite restaurant, and I took her out dancing. She always loved dancing with me even though I am usually the worst dancer on the dance floor. At home, we had a nightcap and went to bed. The next morning was luxurious. We lay in bed kissing and cuddling for hours. I loved the way the sunlight caressed her face and how shiny her golden hair was lit up in the morning light. I was so thankful to have this life with her. When I could peel myself away, I went downstairs to make breakfast. Coffee, orange juice, French toast with fresh berries, all her favorite things. And just as I was drizzling maple syrup on top, Nadia came downstairs carrying a suitcase. She said she had to leave for a while. She needed a break. She was going to stay with her parents. I just stood there with my jaw dropped, still holding the maple syrup. I couldn't speak. I couldn't comprehend what was happening.*

*One minute she was on top of me and the next she was packing her bags? Why? And when I was finally able to get that word out… "why?"… she offered no explanation. Nothing at all. Just "trust* me" and "please don't make this harder than it needs to be". I stood there like a chump and watched her leave me. A week later she changed her social media profiles back to her maiden name. A week after that she sent her parents to our house to collect her things. A month after that, she moved to a different city where she apparently moved in with some guy she met when I was away on business two months earlier.

Needless to say, once I finally grasped what had actually happened, I was beyond broken. Was the whole thing just one big lie? Was I just being blind? How stupid was I, how stubborn had I been, that I had refused to listen to my friends' and family's words of warning? The whole thing was just awful. Around that time, I was a real mess. I was drinking every night, I had a few meaningless rebounds, but none of those things made it any easier. I was spinning out of control. And at the same time, I was constantly trying to save face. In the office, running into people on the street... every time someone unknowingly asked, "How's Nadia?" my stomach knotted up and churned. What could I even tell these people? I hadn't made sense of it myself.

After a while, when the grief still wouldn't shift I decided to take a little time off. I booked two weeks off work and took myself on a holiday. It wasn't the most fun I've ever had but getting away from home did help me start to recover. I needed to process it all. I needed to feel my feelings and since I couldn't seem to do that at home or at work, getting away was a big help. During that time I also stopped drinking and gave up the desperate rebounds. I cried a lot but tried not to put myself down over it. I mean, I had been blindsided. It felt like a tragedy. It was going to take time to get over it. A year later, our divorce was final, and that stung a little. Seeing her in the courtroom wasn't pleasant. Seeing her being picked up by her new guy outside the courtroom was even worse. I felt pretty pathetic.

Now, two years later, I am still single but happily so. I haven't sworn off love or anything like that, I've just taken some time to focus on me. I have realized that when I'm in a relationship, I tend to give that person all my attention, and that means that I neglect my *own needs sometimes. I have also realized that I need to trust my intuition and not just believe everything I'm being told. I was duped by Nadia, and I don't want that to happen again. I do hope to find love again in the not too distant future, but for now, I'm happy just being me.*

# Dealing With The Horrible Emotions

As horrible as breaking up can be, it can give you an opportunity to treat yourself to a heavy dose of TLC. All of us could benefit from being kinder to ourselves, especially when times are tough. Although it can be strange and unsettling to be on your own at the start, when you learn how to really focus on yourself and take special care of yourself, your healing process should benefit in leaps and bounds. Furthermore, when we take the time to take good care of ourselves, we are stamping out negative thought patterns and giving ourselves a chance to really value ourselves. It is common for people to neglect their own needs and put themselves last. But the more we do that, the less energy and love we are giving to ourselves. And the less attention we keep for ourselves, the more negative self-beliefs we will develop.

When your mind is heavy with loss, implementing a daily self-care routine is exactly what you need to get yourself through the dark days. After a break-up, we all need a chance to feel better about ourselves. We need time to lick our wounds and start rebuilding positive self-beliefs. And because so many people have a hard time *telling* themselves that they deserve more in life, by *showing* themselves that they deserve more, they can cut through any feelings of unworthiness they may have developed as a result of their broken relationship. Similarly, if your ex did things to make you feel bad about yourself while you were together such as treating you like their inferior or speaking abusively towards you, you're going to need to dedicate yourself to a daily self-care routine so that you can come out of this feeling strong and confident.

So what does daily self-care actually mean? Put simply, it means making an active decision to do something nice for yourself every single day. This doesn't have to be something particularly extravagant, although it certainly can be if you like. Mostly what it means is doing something for the sole purpose of your own enjoyment and relaxation. This could be anything from getting a manicure to playing sports. It could be taking a bath, listening to a podcast, or reading a newspaper cover to cover. It can be sitting in a quiet room for thirty minutes, or it could be getting together with an old friend who you haven't seen for a while. It's entirely up to you. The important thing is that you don't use your daily self-care time to multitask. Having a meeting with a friend about a project you're working on is not the same as getting together with a friend to simply catch up. Baking something for your kid's PTA bake sale is not self-care no matter how much you enjoy baking! The purpose of self-care is to lift your mood and strengthen your self-esteem. It's a way of showing yourself that you value yourself. It's a way of give yourself love and care when you need it most.

Knowing your worth and valuing yourself appropriately is beneficial to all walks of life. When we feel good about ourselves, we become better workers, better friends, better lovers, and indeed better at believing in ourselves and our capabilities. These are things that everyone needs regardless of what ails them. Another way that you can better look after your heart and mind is by getting quiet, screen-free time every day. This means switching off your mobile devices, your computer and TV and giving yourself a break from it all. This is especially important if you are the type of person who obsessively checks their social media pages, texts, and emails. When we are constantly contactable, it can drastically increase our stress levels. So too, when we're constantly staring at one screen or another, we are in a state of constant stimulation. Our minds are processing a lot at once these days, and unfortunately, when this is the case, we can develop insomnia, anxiety, mental exhaustion, lowered attention span, heightened impatience, and headaches among other things.

Too much stimulation outside of ourselves also means that we're less likely to listen to our own thoughts. We're less likely to reflect on things, to feel our emotions, and follow our own line of thinking. It's hard to be creative when we're over stimulated, and it can make us short tempered. It's like bombarding our brains with tornados and hurricanes when what we really need is for our brains to be metaphorically resting on a sandy beach soaking up the rays. So think about some ways that you can secure some quiet time for yourself on a daily basis. Think about switching your phone off for an hour before bed and reading a book instead of watching TV. Use your lunch break to sit outside while your phone stays in the office.

Take an hour between work and dinner to lay down and simply listen to your thoughts. There endless ways that we can take better care of ourselves, so be creative with it. The important thing is that you're giving yourself plenty of opportunities to feel your feelings.

We all know that the feelings attached to break-ups are not particularly pleasant. But we also know that if we ignore them, they don't go away. Allowing yourself to feel your feelings is the fastest way to resolve difficult emotions. It's not always going to be easy. You will probably cry, experience anger, and question the meaning of life. But try to remember that your emotions just want to be felt, your thoughts just want to be heard. Allowing that to happen is like giving yourself a gift. It's being your own, patient, best friend.

When negative or harmful thought patterns come into your mind, do your best to resist them. Thinking things such as *"I'm bad at relationships", "I always choose the wrong people", "I'll never find love again", "why would anyone even want to be with me"*, etc. will not be of any assistance to you when you're feeling low.

When thoughts like that do come up, try to stamp them out immediately. Treat yourself as you would treat a friend. Tell yourself that those things are not true. Yes, this is a difficult time, but going through a break-up does not mean that you are broken. It doesn't mean that you are weak or unworthy. These things happen to everyone, and although you are hurting now, you will not hurt forever. Be careful not to use your break-up as a means to think poorly of yourself. This is a time when you need to show yourself how good you are, how strong you are, and how worthy of love you are.

While you are immersing yourself in self-care and quiet time, start thinking about what you really want in a relationship. Are there certain qualities that your ex possessed that are not going to work for you in the future? Are there things that that person was lacking? Do you need to be with someone that respects you more? Do you need more space? Do you need more trust in future relationships, or more open honesty?

We all have different needs so it's important to think about these things for yourself while you have some downtime after your break-up. This can be a great time to think about what you really want out of life. It can be a time to make plans for those things and to start reaching higher. If you aren't in a hurry to start dating again, use this time to start getting the other things you want in your life. Start building the life you want, and reach for your goals no matter how unachievable they may seem. Focus on your passion or on learning new things. The aim is to start looking at your life as a whole. Being single does not mean that you are fractured or incomplete. It is not a fault or a flaw. It's an opportunity to do what's right for *you*.

You have to know what it is that you really deserve. You have to know it, believe in it, and start doing what you can do to get it. Maybe your break-up is a good excuse to reinvent yourself. Maybe having more free time means that you'll be able to put more time into your passions or to learn something new that you've always wanted to try. Think of your break-up as a launch pad in this way. Use it as a tool to move on to bigger and better things.

It's worth noting that it's not always the easiest thing to focus on you if your thoughts are still heavily focused on your ex. For people who experience high levels of empathy and selflessness, it is relatively common to be consumed with concern for them. This can manifest in a number of ways; sometimes feelings of guilt may overcome you, you might constantly think about what they're doing and if they're okay, or you might be genuinely worried about their emotional stability.

This can be extremely difficult to cope with, especially if you were the one who kept things together in your relationship. If you're the one that prepared all the meals, you might genuinely be concerned that your ex might not be eating properly. If your ex doesn't have a lot of close friends, you may feel as though you have abandoned them. It's hard to stop caring for someone you have loved, and it's not something that usually happens overnight. But you know where the danger lies in this regard now. You know what has to be done in order to make that cut.

A lot of people tend to believe that they are the only person who really *knows* their ex, and when this is the case, it can feel like you're tossing them out to the wolves. Who will care for them if not you? Who will listen to them and understand them the way you do? Are they even going to be able to take care of themself?

These are common thought patterns, and they're quite complex. Going from all to nothing can be a real mind bender. And of course, this also relates to those feelings of safety and security. When we lose the security of a relationship, it's hard not to cling to it for dear life. We focus on the other person's needs as a way of holding onto that safety and security. We don't want ourselves or our ex to have to rebuild. The problem is that, as you know, when we focus too much attention on our ex's wellbeing we are denying ourselves the attention that we need for our own wellbeing. The longer we cling to what's left of a relationship, the more delayed our recovery will be as an autonomous individual.

It's not easy to tell yourself to stop caring when feelings of empathy for your ex bubble up. It's not easy to turn away from them completely. Even if your relationship ended in an ugly or traumatic way, you might still have to reprogram your focus so that you can be free of your concerns for them.   This can be an emotional minefield for people who are natural caretakers. When you're used to constantly sending your caring vibes outwards, how can you successfully redirect them inward? Well, first of all, you practice good self-care. Second, you get plenty of quiet time. But what then?

You have to get firm with yourself. You have to tell yourself that your ex is an adult and that they are no longer your problem to fix. You have to tell yourself that it is you that needs the love and attention right now. If you treat other people like gold, you have to start figuring out how to treat yourself the way you're inclined to treat them. And every single time your thoughts tell you to fall back into your old care-taking ways, you have to remind yourself of it all again. When you feel the inclination to text them to see if they're okay, give your phone to a friend or put it in another room until the inclination subsides. Bake a cake, go for a jog, read a book. Do whatever you have to do to get your mind off the subject. Maybe you could text a friend who understands your predicament so they can support you through each passing moment. You have to resolve yourself to breaking those care taking habits and start focusing on yourself instead.

It may be difficult at the start, but the more you learn to focus on yourself, the easier and more enjoyable it will become. What's even better is that when you feel it's time to start meeting new people, you will be able to do so with a much healthier sense of self. When we give ourselves the love, approval, and acceptance that we need, we can withstand the ups and downs of life a lot more easily. Therefore, if you take this time to truly focus on yourself, when it comes to getting back into the dating world, you will be a stronger person who knows what they want and what they deserve. This means that your future relationships will be built on more solid ground than those of your past.

Finally, it's important to mention the negative effects your relationship may have had on you. This is especially important for people who were in harmful or abusive relationships. When we are with someone who treats us badly, it can have a terrible effect on how we feel about ourselves. If your ex often spoke to you in a demeaning way, it is very possible that your own self-beliefs may have been altered as a result of that. So too, if you were with someone who lied or betrayed you, you may find it hard to trust people, and you might feel as though you're not worth more than that.

If your ex struggled with addiction or another type of harmful behavior, it might have really done a number on you. In cases such as these, it is extremely important to give yourself time to heal and gain strength. When someone has had power over you, it is natural to find it hard to regain that power for yourself. If you were in an abusive relationship - regardless of whether it involved physical or emotional harm - it could take you a long time to really bounce back. You may benefit from talking to a counselor or attending group therapy with other people who have gone through similar difficulties. It can be really hard to care for yourself when someone else has treated you in a way that made you feel like less of a person.

But you must believe that with time, you will be able to see the good in yourself again. You will be strong again. You will be able to take care of yourself. And eventually, you truly will know how much you're worth.

No one deserves to be in a relationship with someone who disrespects them in any way. Believe that in your heart. Lastly, if you are just out of a harmful relationship, do your very best to take some time to be on your own. It is common for people who are abused or mistreated to begin new relationships quickly and end up in similar circumstances. There are often patterns where things like this are concerned. So in the aftermath of your break-up, try to take a break from dating, and do everything you can to surround yourself with people who treat you with warmth and kindness. Try to look deeper into any harmful patterns you may have and think about why you developed them. Do everything you can to see the good in yourself. Do you everything you can to believe in yourself. Be careful that you are not overly harsh on yourself.

Try not to think about yourself in a negative light. Everyone has things that they could improve upon, but if we insist on thinking or speaking badly of ourselves, that improvement is going to be a lot harder to achieve. However, if you dedicate yourself to practicing daily self-care and you give yourself the time and self-love that you need to recover, you will find greater happiness than you may even think possible.

# Breakup Case Study: Therese

*Jack was the person I trusted most in this world. He had a certain charm, a way of making you believe everything he said. He was supportive and kind. Generous and warm. Before him, I had dated a few guys that had let me down. They hadn't wanted to go out as often as I did. They wouldn't ever make the effort to get to know my friends, and that was something that really mattered to me. My friends mean the world to me, so when Jack came along, I was amazed at how much he wanted to meet them. He showed such an interest in all of them, and naturally, they too were taken with his charm. Finally, a guy who loved socializing as much as I did! And at last, a boyfriend who was happy to hang out with my friends! For a while, I felt like I'd really hit the jackpot, no pun intended.*

*But about six months in, I started feeling apprehensive about Jack. I couldn't really put my finger on what it was that wasn't sitting right with me. In a way, it was like he was just too nice. Like he was too good to be true. He always said what I wanted to hear. And he always seemed a little bit... hyper. Around the same time, one of the girls in my friend group started acting weird around me. She was quieter than usual and wasn't coming out as often with the rest of us. And sure enough, one evening when I was at Jack's house, he went to take a quick shower and left his phone on the coffee table. I wouldn't have looked at it because I had no reason not to trust him, and I'm not really that type of person. But while he was out of the room, he got a message.*

*The name of the sender popped up along with the first line of the text. It was my friend Rachel - the one who had been becoming increasingly distant - and it read "So what's your cover story for tonight?". I felt my stomach drop to my knees. After he'd dressed and showered he came back into the living room and said, "Babe, I totally forgot, I promised the guys I'd come out for a few beers tonight. You don't mind, do you?" And that was how I found out that my boyfriend was sleeping with one of my best friends.*

*I can't even begin to describe what life was like for me over the next few weeks. I honestly don't even remember what I said to him that night. It was a double hit. I was being lied to by two people that I trusted. I was losing a boyfriend and a friend. I had been betrayed. And the messed up thing about it all was that I couldn't even be angry. All I felt was inadequate. Was I not worth more than this? My friends meant everything to me, and now I felt like I couldn't trust any of them. I'd never been cheated on before, and it really destroyed my self-esteem. I really wasn't sure if I'd ever be able to trust anyone again, but more than that, I couldn't stop thinking about what it was about me that was so unlovable. What had I done to deserve to be treated so badly? Had all my friends known about this the whole time?*

*Over the next week, I talked to my friends about it, and they all said they had no idea about Jack and Rachel. Yet at the same time, all of them said that Jack had hit on them at one time or another. When I asked them why they hadn't told me about that stuff, they said they just thought that was his personality and they were just happy that I was happy. The group also refused to cut Rachel out of the group and that hurt so bad. It was like one day I had this great life with all these great people in it, and the next day I had none of it. Nothing. The loss was unbearable.*

*After Jack, it took me a long time to start dating again. I had trust issues, and I needed to work on my confidence. Since the whole thing happened, I was riddled with self-doubt and wary of letting anyone else get close to me. But with time, a lot of the pain subsided. I never spoke to Jack or Rachel again, but I did manage to repair the relationships with my other friends for the most part. Things will never be the same with us as a group now because they have to choose between me and her every time we all want to go out somewhere. Plus, I realized that they really didn't value me the way I needed to be valued. It's been hard finding a new group of friends, but I try to meet new people as much as I can.*

*I am dating again now, but I've realized that I need to take things a lot more slowly in order to trust people. But I know that that's normal considering what happened to me. The good thing is that I know myself better now and I think I know what to look out for. I've been a lot more straightforward with my needs when seeing new people and that has given me a sense of control over things which really helps. Most importantly, I have realized that what happened with Jack was not even about me. I didn't do anything wrong to drive him into the arms of another woman nor was I unloveable. I made a bad judgment call, and I got played. It hurt, but I have survived.*

# Moving On With Your Life!

When you're going through a break-up, it can feel like your world has turned upside down. If your relationship was long-term or if you've been in a number of relationships consecutively, the idea of being single can be pretty terrifying. When we're used to being a part of a couple, learning how to be alone again can be pretty brutal. But it really doesn't have to be. Getting the chance to rediscover your autonomy can actually be really good for the soul. It can lead you to develop increased confidence and higher self-esteem. Being single can help you realize what you're really capable of. In time, you may realize more about who you are and what your real needs are. People change over the course of time. Our experiences and our relationships with others will continue to influence us for as long as we live. And there's something quite exciting about that. Knowing that you will always have the opportunity to grow and change means that there is always hope in your future.

As you know, times of change and transition can be seriously challenging. There will be ups and downs, times of stress and times of relief. Getting back on your feet can take time and patience. Relationships are complicated and getting over them can add even further complication. Of course, you will have some logistical things to work out; especially if you have children or you shared a home with your ex. And thinking about things like that can be overwhelming when your heart is broken. When you're feeling low, simply getting up for work in the morning can feel like too much. No one feels particularly strong or capable when they are carrying around a heavy heart. It's important that you bear this in mind so that you're not too hard on yourself when it feels like you can't accomplish much of anything without difficulty.

This is why it's best to give yourself some time to recover before you start putting pressure on yourself to move on and rebuild your life. Naturally, everyone will need different amounts of recovery time, and this depends on the length of the relationship, the circumstances which led to the break-up, and your own personal response to loss. While some people may find that they can continue to do things as they normally would right away, others may find themselves in a deep state of depression. There is no right or wrong when it comes to your emotions. And unfortunately, there is no set amount of time, no exact expiration date by which you can be certain your pain will recede. So do keep this in mind if you are still in the early stages of the grieving process. Giving yourself time to feel is just as important as rebuilding your life, and you may find that by giving yourself the time to process your emotions, you will bounce back even quicker.

When you are ready to start moving on, you might still feel down. You might find that certain things trigger your emotions; little things that remind you of your ex like certain scents or inside jokes. When these things come up, you may still get pangs of sadness. You may still cry here and there, or you may want to avoid certain places and things that remind you of your ex. All of this is normal, and all of these things will pass with time. Similarly, the world can be a bit cruel when it comes to being single, and it's important to build an emotional defensive wall around yourself and your new circumstances. You may notice that the word *single* often carries a negative connotation. It carries the weight of failure. It's as though *single* means that something is *wrong*. As though you are only half of a person if you're not coupled up. TV, magazines, and the internet will happily deliver constant reminders of the fact that you are no longer part of a couple.

Love is everywhere when it's not in your life. Every show you watch, every book you read, everything in your social media feed will suddenly be about marriage and babies. It can feel like being repeatedly reminded of something you're trying to move beyond. Your friends and family, even when they mean well, are likely to say things like, *"Don't worry, you'll find the right person soon!"* or *"You just wait. Mr or Mrs Right is still out there for you!"*, etc. And even though they may be trying to help, what they are actually doing is instilling the belief within you that you are now somehow incomplete. That being single is just a temporary blip, and soon you'll be back on your feet. But is there any reason you can't get back on your feet as an autonomous being? Is there anything really wrong with becoming an independent individual?

Yes, your friends might encourage you to get back out there and meet new people. You'll suddenly start getting emails from every dating site there is, trying to tempt you into getting back in the game when you might not be ready to. And with every hit, you will be subconsciously led into the belief that being single is wrong, that it's not good enough, and that you will not be complete until you fill the void of your ex. But there is such power to be found in being on your own for a while. The sense of self and the levelheadedness that can bloom as a result of taking some time out is incredible. I mean, doesn't it make sense to take a little break and focus on you for a while? Doesn't it make sense to wait until you feel strong before diving back into the dating pool? The more time we spend on our recovery, the more likely we are to have healthier lasting relationships in the future. This is because we're giving ourselves time to actually learn more about ourselves and our own needs.

When we're 100% clear on what it is that we want from a relationship, we are far more likely to choose the right person, set appropriate boundaries right from the start, and maintain positive self-beliefs throughout the relationship. We are likely to be a better partner. The clearer we are about our own needs, the more likely we are to get them. The more we know what we don't want, the more able we will be to recognize the signs of those things when dating in the future. At the end of the day, the stronger you are in who you are, and the more capable you are of living as an autonomous being, the more levelheaded and resilient you will become. This is a fantastically positive side of being single. And it's not the only one.

Being single means that you get to be selfish. It means you that you can create a wonderful new world that's all your own. The best way to deal with change is to embrace it. Expect the unexpected. Anticipate that there will be ups and downs. You may need to rewrite your routine. You may have to learn some new skills. For instance, if you're not used to living alone anymore, you will have plenty of hurdles to jump. You may need to learn how to cook or how to do DIY jobs around the house. You might find that for the first few months, you just can't keep on top of all the household chores if you used to share them with your ex. But if you let yourself embrace these things, they will be much easier to cope with. Your house might have to be a mess for a while until you can figure things out. You might need to ask a friend for help or hire people to help with the garden or walking the dog. You might feel totally swamped and overwhelmed with all the new pressure on you, and that's okay.

It might be tough for a while, but eventually, you will realize your true strength, and that's when things are going to get really good. Try to look at your new life as an opportunity and something to treasure. There will be times of struggle and frustration, but there will also be times of triumph and pride. Try to hold onto the potential for those positive feelings and self-beliefs as you transition into your new life. Prove to yourself that you can do this. Prove to the world that being single can actually be pretty great. You have not failed. You are not half a person. You are a strong, competent, and *complete* individual. Know that in your heart. And each time you accomplish something that you thought you couldn't do, give yourself credit. Reward yourself when you persevere. Be your own cheerleader whenever you can.

Take some time to think about who you are. Think about who you were before your relationship and who you might be in the future. Accept that you will have changed, as human beings tend to do, over time. Your relationship may have altered the way you think and feel about yourself. You may have developed some new skills or personality traits. You may have developed new fears or worries. You may find that you're less confident about things that you were once more confident about or vice versa. In the future, you are likely to find out even more about yourself. Your recent break-up may cause you to be more cautious or guarded with new people. And hopefully, as you bounce back and start to rebuild your life as a single person, you will develop some new strengths and a deeper understanding of who you are and what you really deserve out of life.

Cherish everything that you have learned through your relationships with other people. Never forget the positive things, and do your best to turn away from the negative. You are at the beginning of the next chapter in your life now, and I wish you the very best. I hope that you will enter this new phase with your head held high.

You *can* overcome whatever life throws your way, just as you have overcome difficulties in the past. Believe in your strength and believe in the goodness in your heart. All good things come to those who wait.

*"A fresh start. A new chapter in life waiting to be written. New questions to be asked, embraced, and loved. Answers to be discovered and then lived in this transformative year of delight and self-discovery. Today carve out a quiet interlude for yourself in which to dream, pen in hand. Only dreams give birth to change."*
**Sarah Ban Breathnach**

## If You Have The Time, Could You Do Me A Favor?

Thank you so much for checking out my book.

I sincerely hope you got value from it. I hope it allows you to get over your breakup and to start a new life. Breakups are never easy and one book can never make all the pain just disappear, but I *really* hope I was able to give you some hope and a direction forward.

If you liked this book could you possibly taking 60 seconds to write a quick review about this book on Amazon?

Thank you!
Your support is much appreciated.
Rachel Adamson.

Manufactured by Amazon.ca
Bolton, ON

12998066R00052